The battles of the Old Testament

A brief expositional guide to the crucial conflicts of the Old Testament and the spiritual lessons for today

Digby B. Williams

DayOne

First published in Great Britain in 2021 by
Day One, Ryelands Road, Leominster, HR6 8NZ
Email: sales@dayone.co.uk
Website: www.dayone.co.uk

British Library Cataloguing in Publication Data available

ISBN: 978-1-84625-771-1

Cover design by Kathryn Chedgzoy

Printed by 4edge

Dedication

To my wife, Linda, for her constant support and encouragement throughout the whole process of this book.

CONTENTS

INTRODUCTION

War is a major theme in the Old Testament. The reason for this lies in the fact that God Himself took a vital role in every area of Israel's life. As a nation, it was subject to the difficulties and conflicts that were common to all other nations. But the unique difference between Israel and the other nations, was that God had entered into a covenant with them and, as such, they were regarded as His 'treasured possession'. Moses describes Israel's privileged position in these words: 'For you are a holy people to the LORD your God, and the LORD has chosen you to be a people for Himself, a special treasure above all the peoples who are on the face of the earth' (Deut. 14: 2).

It is this truth that explains God's pledge to fight their battles, and to drive out their enemies before them. But the people God had chosen were not to think or imagine it was because of any virtue or righteousness in themselves, that God was acting in this way to secure their preservation, or the land which He had promised to them. The Lord's purpose, as stated by Moses, was twofold: firstly, to deal with the wickedness of the nations who had inhabited the land in previous times and, secondly, to fulfill the promises He had made to Abraham, Isaac and Jacob (Deut. 9:4–6).

The nation's existence and preservation, therefore, became God's supreme care and responsibility and their enemies and battles were seen as His also. When Moses outlined the principles of Israel's warfare, he made it clear that the nation would not fight on its own, but with God at their side:

> When you go out to battle against your enemies, and see horses and chariots and people more numerous than you, do not be afraid of them; for the LORD your God is with you, who brought you up from the land of Egypt. So it shall be, when you are on the verge of battle, that the priest shall approach and speak to the people. And he shall say to them, 'Hear, O Israel: Today you are on the verge of battle with your enemies. Do not let your heart faint, do not be afraid, and do not tremble or be terrified because of them; for the LORD your God is He who goes with you, to fight for you against your enemies, to save you (Deut. 20:1–4).

However, Israel's victory in battle was not unconditional. Deliverance came when trust and loyalty to the Lord were actively present among His people. But when Israel trusted in 'horses and chariots' and failed to look to God, failure and defeat were often the outcome, and were seen as God's punishment for Israel's lack of faith. This is very much the theme of the Book of Judges.

This brief study of the Battles of the Old Testament is limited in its scope. For instance, I have not included topographical details, or maps and photographs indicating where battles took place. My main objective has been to lay emphasis on the way faith and victory were joint elements in Israel's success—and unsuccess and defeat when faith was absent. The Christian now lives in a new realm and 'walk[s] in the Spirit' (Galatians 5:25), and his warfare is not 'against flesh and blood, but against principalities, against powers, against the rulers of the darkness of this age, against spiritual hosts of wickedness in the heavenly places' (Eph. 6:12). But the vital principles of trust and obedience to God's Word, still have an essential role to play in the spiritual warfare in which the Christian is engaged. It is for this reason, in particular, that the battles of the Old Testament can be profitable for study and reflection.

Abraham's battle to rescue Lot

Abraham's battle to save Lot

(Genesis 14:1–24)

Setting the scene

This first recorded battle in the Old Testament occurred early in Abraham's history, while he was still being referred to as 'Abram'—not yet having received the covenant name, Abraham, meaning 'father of nations' or multitudes (Gen. 17:1–5). The 'battle of the kings' took place in the Valley of Siddim, a valley named only in Gen. 14:3. Its location today would be to the south end of the Dead Sea. It was a place renowned for its bitumen pits and later named 'Asphaltites' by the Romans.

Lot's capture and rescue

Lot, Abram's nephew, had been caught up in a local war between two sets of tribal rulers. Chedorlaomer, the king of Elam (a country east of Babylonia), headed the one group—a coalition consisting of three kings named Amraphel, Arioch and Tidal, all from the region of Mesopotamia (14:1). These kings marched against the five kings of the Dead Sea area: Bera, Birsha, Shinab, Shemeber and Bela. For twelve years these five kings had paid tribute to Chedorlaomer but, in the thirteenth year, they united together in rebellion against their overlords in the North (14:4). A year later, they paid heavily for their defiance. Chedorlaomer and the coalition of kings swept down the 'King's Highway', east of Jordan, to the region of Sodom and Gomorrah. A decisive battle took place in the Valley of Siddim, resulting in a humiliating defeat for the five kings of Canaan. Some of these petty rulers were driven into the bitumen pits, and the others fled in confusion (14:8–10). The cities of the Plains were plundered, and the retreating armies carried their populace away. In every war there are always innocent victims, and Lot and his family became casualties in this one.

Abram hears of Lot's capture

News of Lot's abduction reached Abram through an escapee, who brought word of the disastrous events concerning the cities of Sodom and Gomorrah. He reacted swiftly, by arming his 318 servants, and pursuing the abductors as far as Dan, the most northerly city in Israel. Dividing his men into two companies, he attacked Chedorlaomer at night, taking advantage of both the cover of darkness and the element of surprise. Recovering the spoils of Sodom and, more importantly, Lot, his family and possessions, he made his way back to the cities of the Plain (14:13–16).

Abram and Melchizedek

On entering the Valley of Shaveh, near the city of Salem, (also known as Jerusalem), Abram was met by the priest-king Melchizedek. This mysterious figure offered him bread and wine, and blessed him in the name of the Lord (14:18–20; see also Hebrews 7:1–4). He was then met by a second prominent figure, the king of Sodom, who offered him the spoils that he had recovered from his victorious campaign to rescue Lot. But both Abram and his men refused to accept as much as a 'thread to a sandal strap', so none would infer it was the king of Sodom that had made Abram rich (14:21–23).

Points for reflection

1] Abram's attitude towards Lot is an example of that brotherly love of which Christ speaks in the Gospel of John: 'This is My commandment, that you love one another as I have loved you' (John 15:12). Abram might have taken a very different attitude to the plight of Lot. He could have reasoned that Lot deserved such a fate—after all, had he not foolishly chosen to live in such a notoriously wicked place such as Sodom? Yet Abram, acting with great compassion and selfless concern for his nephew, risked his own life to rescue him. He bore no grudge and harbored no bitterness towards Lot, and God gave him a resounding victory.

Paul, writing to the Galatians, makes it quite clear as to the way we are to respond to anyone who has been 'overcome by some sin': 'Brethren, if a man is overtaken in any trespass, you who are spiritual restore such a one in a spirit of gentleness, considering yourself lest you also be tempted' (Gal. 6:1). We may be tempted to say to such a person, 'I told you so,' or, 'It serves you right for getting into this mess.' This, however, was not the spirit that characterized Abram or Paul. Nor was it the spirit of the One who was 'before Abraham' (John 8:58), who came from the highest glory to rescue undeserving sinners by suffering death on the cross: 'Greater love has no one than this, than to lay down one's life for his friends' (John 15:13).

2] A further exemplary attitude seen in Abram is the way he reacted to his outstanding victory and achievement in rescuing Lot. This is seen in two ways:

Firstly, his refusal to accept a reward from the ungodly king of Sodom. Undoubtedly, the ministry of Melchizedek had prepared him to face the subtle temptation of becoming rich by receiving 'goods' from such a source. Melchizedek had reminded Abram that God was the 'Most High, Possessor of heaven and earth' (14:19). In his reply to the king of Sodom, Abram quotes these same words, saying, 'I have raised my hand to the LORD, God most High, the Possessor of heaven and earth, that I will take nothing, from a thread to a sandal strap, and that I will not take anything that is yours ... (14:22, 23). Because of this great truth concerning the God of heaven and earth, Abram did not need to receive the riches of a corrupt city and its king. The Lord Himself would be his provider. Jesus tells us to 'seek first the kingdom of God and His righteousness, and all these things shall be added to you' (Matt. 6:33). Millions every week fill in their lottery tickets, hoping to become rich beyond their wildest dreams. But should we, as God's children, be swept along by such desires or by such methods of becoming rich, when our heavenly Father knows how to meet all our needs?

Secondly, Abram resisted the temptation to boast in his success in defeating Lot's abductors. It would have been easy for Abram and his men to glory in their triumph over such a mighty enemy. And again, it was the ministry of Melchizedek which helped to keep Abram humble. His words reminded Abram of what God had done, and not what Abram had done: 'And blessed be God Most High, Who has delivered your enemies into your hand' (Gen. 14:20). Abram recognized that he had conquered the four kings by the power of God and, therefore, to receive any acclamation or reward from the king of Sodom would have been inappropriate and wrong. We can only remain humble by constantly remembering that we are reliant upon God's grace and goodness in every realm of life.

3] We have a greater High Priest than Melchizedek, whose grace, wisdom and power, enables us to conquer the temptations of the 'prince of the power of the air' (Eph. 2:2). The writer to the Hebrews wonderfully summarizes the eternal Priesthood of the Lord Jesus Christ: 'Also there were many priests, because they were prevented by death from continuing. But He, because He continues forever, has an unchangeable priesthood ... For such a High Priest was fitting for us, who is holy, harmless, undefiled, separate from sinners, and has become higher than the heavens'

(Heb. 7:23–24, 26). Just as Abram's conduct before the king of Sodom was guided and influenced by Melchizedek, so must our behaviour before an unbelieving world be controlled by the One who is the King of all kings!

> Before the throne of God above
> I have a strong, a perfect plea,
> A great High Priest, whose Name is 'Love',
> Whoever lives and pleads for me.
> (Charitie Lees Bancroft/De Chenez, 1841–1923)

Chapter 1

Battles of Israel en route to Canaan

Moses and the Battle of Rephidim

(Exodus 17: 8–16)

Setting the scene

Moses and the children of Israel had reached a place called Rephidim ('Plains') on their journey through the Wilderness of Sin. It was here that Israel complained because of a lack of water, and Moses called the place 'Massah' ('testing') and 'Meribah' ('contention'), as a result of their murmuring. (Exod. 17:1–7) It was here also, that a battle was fought with Israel's enemies, the Amalekites, who were a branch of the Edomite race and descendants of Amalek, the grandson of Esau (Gen. 36:12). These people ranged over a wide area of territory, roughly known as the Southland or Negeb. They were probably nomadic and particularly hostile towards the children of Israel.

The attack

The Amalekites attacked the rear ranks and stragglers in Israel's company, hoping to impede and block their progress through the Wilderness. In all probability, the Amalekites had become suspicious of Israel's presence in an area which was unusually fertile and, in their view, not big enough to support the grazing of two peoples at the same time. Their strategy to attack the 'tired and weary' (Deut. 25:17–19) at Israel's rear flanks merited the divine judgement. Moses was to make a solemn record of Amalek's act of wickedness as a testimony against them, and also to give a prophetic Word from the Lord: '... the

Lord has sworn: the Lord will have war with Amalek from generation to generation' (Exod. 17:14, 16).

The response

Moses summoned Joshua to select an army to go out and fight against the Amalekites. The following day, he positioned himself, along with Aaron and Hur, at the top of a hill overlooking the plain of Rephidim. Down below, the two armies met in battle and the advantage oscillated between each side, sometimes in Israel's favour and at other times in their enemy's favour. When Moses held high the staff of God, Israel gained the upper hand but, when his hands sank down, the scene changed and Israel were beaten back. Aaron and Hur saw the strain on Moses to stand with arms uplifted, so a stone was brought for him to sit on, and both men supported his arms and kept him in that position until the sky grew dark. The outcome was that Israel's enemy was utterly disabled by Joshua's forces.

Points for reflection

Both in the attack by Amalek and in the victory won by Israel, there are spiritual lessons for the Church and the individual Christian.

The assault

1] Why did Amalek attack Israel? Was it simply because they were intruding into their territory and were a threat to their wells? This may have been the cause on one level, but the Scriptures give us a deeper reason for their opposition: a hostility towards the God of Israel (Deut. 25:18). Amalek came and fought against the children of Israel, not just because he hated them as intruders, but because he hated them as the people of God. The devil was clearly behind this attack against God's chosen people and, just as he tried to hinder and oppose Israel's progress to the 'land of promise' then, so today he seeks to thwart the spiritual progress of the Church and every individual child of God. Whether it is in the area of evangelism, leadership or prayer, the devil will seek to impede and disrupt the work of the gospel. Paul, writing to the Christians at Thessalonica, explained how he, along with Timothy and Silvanus, had wanted to visit them but he says, 'Satan hindered us' (1 Thes. 2:18). We are exhorted to 'Put on the whole armour of God, that you may be able to stand against the wiles of the devil.' If we are to 'withstand' his wiles, our strength needs to be in the 'Lord and in the power of His might' (Eph. 6:10–13).

2] The subtle and cunning manner of the attack at Rephidim is also a reminder of the way Satan often works to hinder the growth of the Church. Amalek attacked the weak and weary among Israel's number. The devil, likewise, is always quick to exploit the weak links in the Church's armour. Whether it is compromise or corruption of the truth, lukewarmness or spiritual pride, the Church always needs to be on its guard. The seven churches mentioned, in the opening chapters of the Book of Revelation, bear record to the manifold ways in which the devil seeks to impede the growth of the Church (see the messages to the churches in Rev. 2 & 3).

But, of course, Amalek was not only interested in attacking the vulnerable sections of Israel, but also the best of Israel's fighting force (Exod. 17:8). The enemy of the Church will also seek to exploit the strengths of any particular church. A church may be known for its ministry and enjoy the respect and admiration of other churches. It may, on the other hand, be a church which seems to have unlimited funds and gifts, and has a busy programme of activities. But it is at that point that both churches need to be on their guard against the temptation of saying, 'I am rich, have become wealthy, and have need of nothing ...' but, in reality, they do not know that they '... are wretched, miserable, poor, blind, and naked' (Rev. 3:17).

3] A further point about Amalek's attack against Israel is that it came soon after they had received the miraculous provision of water (Exod. 17:5–6). Here, the whole company of Israel, was blessed with a manifestation of God's power and faithfulness. The devil may attack after times of blessing when we least expect it. Paul, writing to the Corinthian church, assured them that he had forgiven one of their number, '... lest Satan should take advantage of us; for we are not ignorant of his devices' (2 Cor. 2:11).

The apostle knew that, if he or others had withheld their forgiveness for this particular brother, Satan would have used this as a means of discrediting his God-given authority as an apostle of Christ, which in turn would have discredited the message he preached. We too, must not be ignorant of his many devices to bring the gospel into disrepute, by harbouring grudges against our fellow believers.

The victory

1] The first thing to note, is that Israel did not gain the victory over Amalek without a fight (Exod. 17:9). It was different at the Red Sea when Moses commanded the people to 'Stand still, and see the salvation of the LORD ...' (Exod. 14:13). There at the Red Sea the Israelites were utterly defenceless against Pharaoh's army of chariots and horsemen. The Lord never expects us to do the impossible! He equips us with all the necessary means to 'fight the good fight of faith' (1 Tim. 6:12) and expects us to 'take up' and to 'put on the whole armour of God' (Eph. 6:13, 11).

But when a situation overwhelms us, He promises to make a way of escape:

> But God is faithful, who will not allow you to be tempted beyond what you are able, but with the temptation will also make the way of escape, that you may be able to bear it (1 Cor. 10:13).

2] Israel's triumph over Amalek, however, has its true

explanation in the activity of Moses, Aaron and Hur. While Joshua and his forces fought the physical battle in the valley below, Moses was engaged in the spiritual battle on the hill. With the staff of God in his hand (a symbol of divine intervention) and his arms held up high in prayer, Moses interceded for God's people as they struggled to overcome the enemy. The commonly used phrase, 'prayer support', has a literal ring to it in this incident! Moses could not have prevailed alone; he needed the support of Aaron and Hur. How much more do we, as the soldiers of Christ, need the support of the prayers of one another as we fight in this valley below. But let us be confident that our prayers are heard at the throne of heaven. Alfred Lord Tennyson, the great English poet, said, 'More things are wrought by prayer than this world dreams of.'[1]

> Restraining prayer we cease to fight;
> prayer makes the Christian's armour bright;
> and Satan trembles when he sees
> the weakest saint upon his knees.
> (William Cowper, 1731–1800)

Chapter 2

Israel's defeat by the Amalekites

(Numbers 14:39–45)

Setting the scene

The futile and presumptuous attempt by the children of Israel to invade the territory of the Amalekites and the Canaanites is the third recorded conflict in the Old Testament. Israel suffered a humiliating defeat, not because they failed to fight, but because they failed to obey God.

The spies give a bad report of the land

The Israelites had left Egypt and arrived at Mount Sinai, having successfully fought off a challenge by the Amalekites at the plains of Rephidim (Exod. 17:8–16; 19:1). A number of days after leaving Mt Sinai, Moses was instructed by the Lord to send twelve spies into Canaan in order to survey and explore the land. They were to find out '... whether the people who dwell in it are strong or weak, few or many ... whether the cities they inhabit are like camps or strongholds ...'. They were also to find out if the land contained forests or not and were also instructed to bring back a sample of fruit from the land (Num. 13:17–20). The spies returned and acknowledged that, in reality, it was a richly fertile land, a land that 'truly flows with milk and honey'. But as they continued their report the news became increasingly gloomy. Ten of the spies spoke of the cities and their fortifications which were 'very large'; they spoke of the people themselves being 'strong', and if that was not enough, they even saw the 'descendants of Anak' there—or, as the Living Bible translation puts it, they 'saw the Anakim giants there!' (Num. 13:28, 29). But their report moved from being something simply factual, to something imaginary and alarming: 'The land ... is a land that devours its inhabitants ...' (v. 32).

The effect of this report upon the congregation of Israel was devastating. Dismay and fear soon turned into anger and bitter criticism against Moses and, more seriously, against God Himself: 'Why has the LORD brought us to this land to fall by the sword ...' (Num. 14:3). They then planned to replace Moses with a leader who would take them back to Egypt. Joshua and Caleb responded by tearing their clothes in consternation, and tried to quell this sudden rebellion by affirming that the land was all that God had promised it would be—an 'exceedingly good land'. They assured the people that if God was pleased with them, He would bring them safely there and give it to them as a possession. But they were not to rebel or collapse in fear because the Lord's presence would secure their success over their enemies. Sadly, Caleb's and Joshua's powerful reasoning failed to win over the people, and in blind anger they all talked of stoning both men (Num. 14:6–10).

Moses intercedes for the people

The Lord then revealed to Moses His displeasure with the people's rejection and unbelief, and threatened to disinherit and destroy them with a plague (Num.

14:11–12). What follows, is Moses' earnest prayer for the people, and God's gracious answer to pardon the iniquity of His recalcitrant people. However, because of their rebellion and unbelief, that generation would perish in the desert, and their ancestors would enter the Promised Land. Only Caleb and Joshua of that generation would see the land which God had sworn to their fathers. Furthermore, their punishment for putting God to the test and despising His Word, would be a forty-year journey through the Wilderness—a number that corresponded to the number of days the spies spent reconnoitering the land (see vv. 11–38).

The people's presumption

In v. 39, Moses relates to the children of Israel all that God had said to him concerning the penalty for their unfaithfulness and sin. They react by greatly mourning over their behaviour but, unfortunately, their mourning is short-lived because they announce to Moses their intention of going up 'to the place which the LORD has promised ...'(v. 40). Moses does his best to warn them of their foolishness: firstly, they will be breaking a clear command of the Lord (v. 41; see also v. 25). Secondly, if they do try to take things into their own hands, they will not 'succeed' and will be defeated by their enemies (vv. 41–42). But thirdly, and most importantly, the Lord will not be with them (vv. 42–43).

Their reaction to this warning was a stubborn refusal to listen, and a reckless attempt to fight against the Canaanites. Their humiliating defeat is recounted by Moses years later:

> And the LORD said to me, 'Tell them, "Do not go up or fight, for I am not among you; lest you be defeated before your enemies." So I spoke to you; yet you would not listen, but rebelled against the command of the LORD, and presumptuously went up into the mountain. And the Amorites who dwelt in that mountain came out against you and chased you as bees do, and drove you back from Seir to Hormah. Then you returned and wept before the LORD, but the LORD would not listen to your voice nor give ear to you (Deut. 1:42–44).

Points for reflection

1] Israel's presumption shows the perversity of sin. When they are exhorted to 'go up and take possession' of the land, they say 'no, let us return to Egypt'. When the Lord says, 'You shall not come into the land', they say, 'Here we are, we will go up to the place which the LORD has promised.' When they should have gone forward, they wanted to turn back. When they should have turned back, they insisted on going forward! Paul speaks of his generation as a 'crooked and perverse generation', and he exhorts the Christians at Philippi to be 'blameless and harmless', and as the children of God to 'shine as lights in the world' (Phil. 2:15). Our generation is no different from any other generation in the past, and our calling as believers remains exactly the same: to be light bearers of the truth of the gospel.

2] The presence of the Lord with His people is the secret of their power and courage but, alternately, the withdrawal of His presence leaves them fearful and confused. Samson's remarkable strength and courage remained with him throughout his years as Israel's judge, until he succumbed to Delilah's charms and enticements. He mistakenly thought that nothing would change when his locks had been shaved off and foolishly said, when awaking from his sleep, '"I will go out as before, at other times, and shake myself free!" But he did not know that the LORD had departed from him' (Judges 16:20). While we thank God that He will never forsake us, or take His Spirit from us, we must realize that sin always robs us of the power and consciousness of His presence.

3] As churches and individual believers we should not attempt to do the Lord's work in our own strength, and by our own wisdom. Spiritual work requires spiritual power: '... without Me [says our Lord] you can do nothing'. He means, of course, nothing of any spiritual value or worth (John 15:5). The positive to this is Paul's affirmation: 'I can do all things through Christ who strengthens me'

(Phil. 4:13). When he was about to enter and preach in the depraved city of Corinth, Paul acknowledged that he was with them 'in fear, and in much trembling,' and yet his preaching demonstrated the fact that God's power rested on him. The result was that their faith was not through the wisdom of men, 'but in the power of God' (1 Cor. 2:3–5).

4] This whole incident sadly reveals how the children of Israel were governed, not by faith, but by a dark and depressing unbelief. It led them to despise their redemption from Egypt and to provoke the Lord who had rescued them from bondage. Their unbelief also blinded them to the gracious reasoning of Joshua and Caleb and, finally, it was the cause of them being barred from entering 'His rest':

> Now with whom was He angry forty years? Was it not with those who sinned, whose corpses fell in the wilderness? And to whom did He swear that they would not enter His rest, but to those who did not obey? So we see that they could not enter in because of unbelief (Heb. 3:17–18).

Chapter 3

Israel's victory over three Amorite kings

(Numbers 21:1–3, 21–35)

Setting the scene

The three battles recorded in this chapter, were battles that Israel fought en route to Canaan. While they may have seemed to be of lesser importance than some of the later conflicts, the two battles against King Sihon and King Og stayed in the national memory for generations afterwards. For instance, the Psalmist celebrated the occasion by attributing the victory to the Lord:

> He defeated many nations and slew mighty kings—Sihon king of the Amorites, Og king of Bashan, and all the kingdoms of Canaan—and gave their land as a heritage, a heritage to Israel His people (Ps. 135:10–12).

Their victory over these kings was also to reverberate throughout the cities of Cannan, especially the walled city of Jericho where Rahab lived. The evidence for this is seen in her testimony to the two Israelite spies who had entered her house:

> I know that the LORD has given you the land.... and that all the inhabitants of the land are faint-hearted .... For we have heard ... what you did to the two kings of the Amorites who were on the other side of the Jordon, Sihon and Og, whom you utterly destroyed (Josh. 2:9–10).

The first battle at Hormah (21:1–3)

Arad, the king who ruled in the South of Canaan was the first Canaanite king to be defeated by the children of Israel. In this sense it was the dawn of a new epoch in their history, the beginning of their conquest of the Promised Land—a pledge of future possession. But Israel were not the aggressors in this conflict. Arad came out to fight against Israel as they approached his territory and managed to take some of them as prisoners. In the previous conflict, where Israel had made a rash and unsuccessful attempt to invade Canaan, there was no prayer and no trust in God. But now, at Hormah, their vow to the Lord speaks of their dependency on God: 'If You will indeed deliver this people into my hand, then I will utterly destroy their cities' (Num. 21:2).

Points for reflection

Just as this battle marked a new era for the children of Israel and a guarantee of their inheritance, so it is with the spiritual battle in the life of every child of God. Paul, writing to the Christians at Ephesus, reminds them that their conversion had marked a new era in their lives, and a guarantee of their eternal inheritance:

> In Him you also trusted, after you heard the word of truth, the gospel of your salvation; in whom also, having believed, you were sealed with the Holy Spirit of promise, who is the guarantee of our inheritance

> until the redemption of the purchased possession, to the praise of His glory (Eph. 1:13–14).

Unlike Israel, our victory over our enemies, sin, death and hell, has not been accomplished by human effort, but by the redeeming work of the Lord Jesus Christ:

> He has delivered us from the power of darkness and conveyed us into the kingdom of the Son of His love, in whom we have redemption through his blood, the forgiveness of sins (Col. 1:13–14).

The second battle against Sihon of Heshbon (21:21–26)

The Amorite kingdom was one of the two principal kingdoms in Cannan—the territory known sometimes as the kingdom of Tyre or Phoenicia (Isa. 23:8). They were merchants of purple dye; the Hebrew name for 'Canaanite' also means 'merchant'. When Israel had arrived at the border of Sihon's territory, they sent messengers to request a right of passage. They sought to assure the King that they would not venture into his vineyards or take water from his wells (Num. 21:22). Instead, they would keep to the 'King's Highway' (probably the road from Damascus to the Gulf of Aqaba). These words of reassurance were ignored by Sihon, who foolishly left his fortified city to engage with Israel in open country at Jahaz (Num. 21:23). But King Sihon not only displayed his foolishness with regard to his military strategy but, more importantly, by refusing Israel to pass peacefully through his territory, thus pitting himself against the God of Israel.

Points for reflection

If men and women today refuse God's offer of peace in the gospel, they too are guilty of great foolishness and ultimate ruin. Paul speaks passionately about this offer of reconciliation in his Second Letter to the Corinthians:

> Now then, we are ambassadors for Christ, as though God were pleading through us: we implore you on Christ's behalf, be reconciled to God. For He made Him who knew no sin to be sin for us, that we might become the righteousness of God in Him (2 Cor. 5:20).

The battle against Og, king of Bashan (Num. 21:33–35)

Israel travelled on to Bashan, an area east of the Sea of Galilee, and fought a battle at Edrei—the city where King Og presided. Again, Israel's enemy was the instigator of this conflict who, like Sihon, was a real threat to Israel's existence. But, as before, God gave His people a resounding victory as He had promised Moses (v. 34).

It is clear from the account of this incident in the Book of Deuteronomy that Og's kingdom was very powerful and, therefore, the significance of this victory is clear from Moses' record of it:

> So the LORD our God also delivered into our hands Og king of Bashan, with all his people .... And we took all his cities at that time; there was not a city which we did not take from them; sixty cities .... All these cities were fortified with high walls, gates, and bars, besides a great many rural towns (Deut. 3:3–5).

This clearly speaks of the divine intervention of the Lord over a potentially forceful and dominant enemy. And, to emphasize this, we have Moses' description of Og himself: 'For only Og king of Bashan remained of the remnant of the giants. Indeed his bedstead was an iron bedstead .... Nine cubits is its length and four cubits its width' (Deut. 3:11).

Points for reflection

1] Giants mean nothing to God. Likewise, the 'giants' which may frighten us, whether they be inward or outward fears—God's grace will be more than sufficient to deal with them.

> Fear not I am with Thee, O be not dismayed!
> For I am thy God, and will still give thee aid;
> I'll strengthen thee, help thee, and cause thee
> to stand,
> Upheld by My righteous, omnipotent hand.'
> ('K' in Rippon's Selection of Hymns, 1787)

Conquest of the Midianites

(Numbers 31:1–12)

Setting the scene

The campaign against the Midianites was by the express command of the Lord: 'And the LORD spoke to Moses, saying: "Take vengeance on the Midianites for the children of Israel"' (Num. 31:1). The key, therefore, to this Israelite attack has to do with divine judgement. Vengeance is always something which belongs to God, rather than men. Paul, writing to the Christians at Rome, makes this clear: 'Beloved, do not avenge yourselves, ... for it is written, "Vengeance is Mine, I will repay," says the Lord' (Rom. 12:19). Most often, in the Old Testament, God's vengeance is seen towards the enemies of God's people. But, in some cases, it is directed against the nation of Israel itself when they have flagrantly disobeyed God's Word and have acted against His will.

The question to ask is, 'Why was God taking vengeance against these particular people, the Midianites?' Well, their general crime consisted of their persistent hostility against the children of Israel (Judg. 6:1–6). But their more specific sin was that they were guilty of luring Israel into pagan worship, which involved religious prostitution (Num. 25:1–3). In participating in pagan sacrifices, the children of Israel had 'yoked' or 'coupled' themselves to Baal. In terms of the covenant with God, they had breached it by their spiritual infidelity. If we think of marital unfaithfulness, Israel had committed adultery;

they had cheated on God. The prophet, Hosea, pinpoints their transgression with these striking words: 'But they went to Baal Peor, and separated themselves to that shame; they became an abomination like the thing they loved' (Hosea 9:10). So, the Midianites had seduced Israel into committing apostasy and the Lord was now about to punish them.

However, there was someone, in particular, behind this apostasy—an individual who is named as having died in this campaign (Num. 31:8). Balaam was co-responsible for causing the Midianite women to induce Israel to 'trespass against the LORD' (Num. 31:16). The words of the Lord Jesus Christ to the church of Pergamos throw light on Balaam's act of treachery:

> But I have a few things against you, because you have there those who hold the doctrine of Balaam, who taught Balak to put a stumbling block before the children of Israel, to eat things sacrificed to idols, and to commit sexual immorality (Rev. 2:14).

The battle (Num. 31:3–8)

Moses ordered each tribe of Israel to select a thousand men to fight against the Midianites. All twelve thousand men were under the leadership of a man called Phinehas, a priest who was the grandson of Aaron. This would have been a fairly small section of Israel's army and would have been chosen as a special task force. It may seem unusual for a priest to be given the role of a commander of a fighting army, but it emphasized the nature of this battle. It was, in reality, the Lord's battle, because He commanded who should be destroyed and who should be spared (Num. 31:14–19). The priestly duty at a time of war was very simple, as outlined in the twentieth chapter of the Book of Deuteronomy:

> So it shall be, when you are on the verge of battle, that the priest shall approach and speak to the people. And he shall say to them, 'Hear, O Israel: Today you are on the verge of battle with your enemies. Do not let your heart faint, do not be afraid, and do not tremble or be terrified because of them; for the LORD your God is He who goes with you, to fight for you against your enemies, to save you' (Deut. 20:2–4).

On this occasion, the priestly leader would have encouraged the troops to realize the Lord was with them and, therefore, the victory would be assured. The five kings of Midian were put to death, along with all the males. The women and children were spared as plunder. However, Moses commanded that only the virgin women could be spared, since they were probably innocent of the obscenities at Baal Peor.

Points for Reflection

1] The land that the children of Israel were to possess had to be a land purged of evil. The conquest of Israel is to be seen in this light. Canaan and its inhabitants would always be a threat to the very existence of God's people, both in terms of their physical and spiritual lives. Because of their sorcery and foul religious practices, they would always be a source of spiritual corruption, which of course they proved to be throughout Israel's history. The message of these conflicts, therefore, is that a holy and loving God must deal justly with all evil.

Those who have been redeemed by Christ's blood, no longer belong to themselves, but to Him who has saved them. We are now the privileged sons and daughters of God, who are being sanctified and purged by His grace from the presence of sin within us. We are to 'put to death' all forms of evil such as 'fornication, uncleanness, passion, evil desire, and covetousness which is idolatry.' And as 'the elect of God', there are certain things which we must 'put off'' and other things which we must 'put on'. We are to 'put off all these: anger, wrath, malice, blasphemy, filthy language out your mouth.' And as 'holy and beloved' we are to 'put on tender mercies, kindness, humility, meekness, long-suffering; bearing with one another, and forgiving one another' (Colossians 3:5–13).

2] One of the great incentives to remain faithful to the

Lord Jesus Christ is to remind ourselves that we are no longer 'married' to the law, but to Him. Our whole position is different, as Paul outlines in his letter to the Christians at Rome: 'Therefore, my brethren, you also have become dead to the law through the body of Christ, that you may be married to another—to Him who was raised from the dead, that we should bear fruit to God' (Rom. 7:4). Our union with Christ liberates us from our old position of being 'under law', to being 'under grace', and brings us into a completely new realm of living, described by Paul as 'newness of life' (Rom. 6:4).

3] As Christians we face many battles in life, such as those things we have mentioned above. Just as the children of Israel were exhorted time and again not to be afraid as they approached their battles, so we, as God's people today, must never succumb to fear. Paul, encouraging his younger co-worker Timothy who may have been prone to fear and timidity, says, 'For God has not given us a spirit of fear, but of power and of love and of a sound mind' (2 Tim. 1:7).

> Fear not, brethren; joyful stand
> On the borders of our land;
> Jesus Christ, our Father's Son,
> Bids us undismayed go on.
> (John Cennick, 1718–55)

Battles in the conquest for Canaan

The Battle of Jericho (1)

(Joshua 5:10–6:5)

Setting the scene

The prelude (1)

Joshua's encounter with the 'Commander of the Lord's army', is the prelude and the deciding factor in Israel's victory at Jericho. Having successfully crossed the River Jordan, Joshua now confronts his greatest challenge, the battle to take Jericho. It must have been a time of exceptional anxiety and suspense for him, since now the weight and burden of leadership lay heavily upon his shoulders. But who better to deal with an apprehensive servant of God, than the Lord Himself! As Joshua surveyed the impregnable walls of Jericho, 'a Man stood opposite him with His sword drawn in His hand.' Not immediately recognizing the stranger, Joshua approached Him with the obvious question: 'Are You for us or for our adversaries?' The reply could not have been more unexpected or astonishing; the answer was: 'No, but as Commander of the army of the Lord I have now come' (Josh. 5:13, 14).

Joshua's response is to fall prostrate in worship before the Lord. In that moment Joshua would probably have realized that the ultimate responsibility for the battle was no longer his. He was ready to receive his orders from the One who would oversee and direct all that would take place: 'What does my Lord say to His servant?' (v. 14). But, before any orders are given, Joshua is reminded of the holiness of his 'Commander'; the very ground upon which he stands is holy and, therefore, as a sign of humility and reverence he must remove his sandals. Now, in a spirit of awesome wonder, Joshua's heart and mind are truly ready to hear and obey the Lord's directions on how he is to fight this battle.

The Lord's first word to Joshua is one of great assurance: 'See! I have given Jericho into your hand, its king and the mighty men of valor' (Josh. 6:2). In the Lord's eyes, defeat had already taken place for Israel's enemies. This is reinforced in the testimony of Rahab to the two Israelite spies: 'I know that the LORD has given you the land, that the terror of you has fallen on us, and that all the inhabitants of the land are fainthearted because of you' (Josh. 2:8).

Points for reflection

In this prelude to the battle of Jericho, there are a few spiritual principles which are there for our help and encouragement as we, as the soldiers of the Lord, 'stand against the wiles of the devil' (Ephesians 6:11).

1] Joshua is to begin the conquest of Canaan at the Lord's feet, in worship and in humble expectancy. 'And Joshua fell on his face to the earth and worshipped ....' This must always be the place where our service for the Lord begins and ends. Elizabeth Charles expresses this so well in one of her hymns:

> Never further than Thy cross,
> Never higher than Thy feet;
> Here earth's precious things seem dross,
> Here earth's bitter things grow sweet.

Here we learn to serve and give,
And, rejoicing, self deny;
Here we gather love to live,
Here we gather faith to die.

2] Holiness in the Christian life is not an 'optional extra'—something we may or may not adopt, as we live out our lives in this world. It is the fundamental requirement for all who have been pardoned and saved by God's grace. 'He has shown you, O man, what is good; and what does the LORD require of you, but to do justly, to love mercy, and to walk humbly with your God?' (Micah 6:8). In a sense, like Joshua, we are all standing on holy ground; we are all under the eye and in the presence of our heavenly Father. We are therefore to 'Pursue peace with all people, and holiness, without which no one will see the Lord' (Heb. 12:14).

3] Joshua is assured that he is about to fight this battle, not from a spirit of defeat and fear, but rather with a confidence that, in Christ, the enemy has been overcome. Our tendency is to magnify the difficulties instead of magnifying the Lord's power to deal with our difficulties.

When Satan tempts me to despair,
And tells me of the guilt within,
Upward I look, and see Him there
Who made an end of all my sin.
(Charitie Lees Bancroft /De Chenez, 1841–1923)

The Battle of Jericho (2)

(Joshua 6:6–27)

Setting the scene

The conquest (2)

Joshua had received intelligence about Jericho's position, its fortifications and its inhabitants, from the two Israelite spies. They had also heard from one of its citizens, Rahab, that the population of Jericho had melted in fear because of their victory over the Amorites. The spies rightly deduced from all that they had heard and seen that, 'Truly the LORD has delivered all the land into our hands, for indeed all the inhabitants of the country are fainthearted because of us' (Joshua 2:24).

The fall of Jericho had nothing to do with military strength or skill. It had, however, everything to do with God's power manifested in response to Israel's faith and obedience. It is not surprising, then, that these two things are the key elements in the destruction of Jericho: 'By faith the walls of Jericho fell down after they were encircled for seven days' (Heb. 11:30).

Jericho is taken.

Now the Lord's instructions to Joshua were not complicated, but they were very unconventional. A procession made up of seven priests carrying trumpets, and other priests carrying the ark, were to march between an advance guard and a rear guard around the city once a day for six days. On the seventh day, the procession was to encompass the city seven times and, on the seventh time, at the sound of a long blast on the trumpets, the people were to shout. The ark was to take the central place in the midst of the armed people. It symbolized God's presence among His people and the blowing of trumpets signified the spiritual nature of this conflict. The people's shout was the means by which God would work mightily to accomplish the destruction of the city's defences. The city walls 'fell down flat' or 'under it' (v. 20), and the collapse of the walls in this particular way gave Israel unhindered access into the city. It has been pointed out that, had the walls collapsed in any other way, the rubble would have been a major obstacle in the path of the advancing army. As it was, the walls sunk miraculously into the earth, thus causing no barrier to Israel's advance.

The Lord's command was that all the inhabitants of Jericho were to be destroyed. Only Rahab and her family were to be saved, as the fulfilment of the promise made by the two spies when they hid in Rahab's house: 'So the men answered her, "Our lives for yours, if none of you tell this business of ours. And it shall be, when the LORD has given us the land, that we will deal kindly and truly with you"' (Josh. 2:14).

Points for reflection

Joshua's command to the people, to be silent as they encircled the city, is both interesting and significant for a number of reasons.

1] Firstly, it marked the difference between the ways of God and the ways of men. Silence is not something that the world advocates to be of great benefit. It prefers noise, razzmatazz and clamour. Think for instance of an election campaign in the USA, which seems to resemble a circus rather than a political campaign. Even on a personal level, quietness and stillness may be more disturbing than refreshing! Isaiah contrasts God's thoughts and ways with the thoughts and ways of man: 'For as the heavens are higher than the earth, so are My ways higher than your ways, and My thoughts than your thoughts' (Isa. 55:9).

2] Secondly, the absence of sound as the people walked around the city would have produced a spirit of expectancy. The Israelites would also have sensed the awesome nature of the occasion, and an air of stillness would have added to the solemn atmosphere. We have all experienced being in a crowd and suddenly everything goes quiet; immediately the environment is changed! The writer of the Book of Ecclesiastes has this advice for believers when they meet for worship in the Lord's house:

> Walk prudently when you go to the house of God; and draw near to hear rather than to give the sacrifice of fools, for they do not know that they do evil. Do not be rash with your mouth, and let not your heart utter anything hastily before God. For

> God is in heaven, and you on earth; Therefore let your words be few (Eccles 5:1–2).

Do we have a spirit of expectancy as we wait to hear God's Word, or does our chatter drown out any expectation that the Lord will speak into our situation and bring light where there may be darkness?

3] Thirdly, the imposed silence on the children of Israel was a test of their faith and obedience. Throughout their wanderings through the wilderness, their fathers had been prone to murmuring and complaining. Now, this new generation would be tested on their willingness to accept Joshua's orders, even though they may not have fully understood them. We can imagine the conversations among some of the people as they arrived back at their camp after each day's march: 'What are we supposed to be achieving by marching around the city in silence? It all seems a waste of time!' But, of course, they were achieving a great deal; simply by obeying God they were honouring Him and would reap the reward of their faithful submission to His Word.

4] But, fourthly, in addition to this, it was also a test of their patience. The march would not just take a day but seven days, and on the seventh day the city would have to be encircled seven times. The Bible often links faith with patience, seeing them as two sides of a coin. James exhorts his readers to 'count it all joy when you fall into various trials, knowing that the testing of your faith produces patience' (James 1:2–3). The writer to the Hebrews warns his readers not to become sluggish but, instead, 'imitate those who through *faith and patience* inherit the promises' (Heb. 6:12).

The campaign against Ai (1)

(Joshua 7:1–9)

Setting the scene

Although the city of Ai (meaning 'ruin') marked the next clear goal in Israel's conquest of Canaan, the plan to take the city smacked more of their initiative than divine guidance. On the advice of the spies that Joshua had sent to 'spy out the country' (v. 2), only a section of the army was sent to attack the city (7:2, 3). This display of over confidence, however, was not the cause of Israel's humiliating defeat, as Joshua was later to find out. The force of three thousand Israelites was driven back and chased down a steep descent towards Shebarim (stone quarries) and in the confusion thirty-six Israelite men lost their lives. Such a crushing and unforeseen defeat caused the 'hearts of the people [to] melt' (v. 5). The irony of this military fiasco was that Israel suffered the same painful experience as the people of Jericho, when their 'hearts melted' and their courage evaporated at the news of Israel's victories (2:11).

Joshua's response to Israel's blunder

Joshua's anguish and sorrow at the news of the defeat is expressed by his actions before the ark of the Lord. His complete dismay is seen as he prostrates himself before the Lord and remains in that contrite position until the evening (7:6). His prayer indicates the agitation of his mind, as he tried to understand the reason for such a setback. His cry to God contains the 'why' of bewilderment:

'Alas, LORD God, why have You brought this people over the Jordan at all—to deliver us into the hand of the Amorites, to destroy us?' (v. 7). It is a prayer that also contains the 'what' of shame and reproach: 'O LORD, what shall I say when Israel turns its back before its enemies? (v. 8). Yet, being a man of God, Joshua's great concern is not for his own reputation as a military leader, but for the Name and glory of God.

The why is answered

The Lord quickly enlightens Joshua as to the true reason for Israel's failure at Ai. Israel had sinned. God's covenant had been violated and that which should have been 'devoted' to the Lord had been stolen and hidden (vv. 10–12). He makes it clear to Joshua that it is not the time for wallowing in grief or self-pity, but rather a time to take firm action and find and punish the one responsible for the offence. Without this, Israel would never again be able to stand against her enemies (v. 12). Joshua wastes no time in bringing the guilty party to light from Israel's ranks. All the people are brought before Joshua, tribe by tribe, family by family, until Achan—the cause of Israel's defeat—is discovered. Joshua then pronounces God's judgement upon him and his family, and the people stone them at the Valley of Achor. With the death of Achan and the destruction of the accursed things (the silver, gold and the Babylonian garment from Jericho) the wrath of God is turned away from Israel.

Points for reflection

1] The defeat at Ai came on the heels of Israel's success at Jericho. No one could have foreseen this unexpected setback at Ai. Spiritual success can often make churches careless and overconfident in their abilities and activities. The writer, John Blanchard, made this poignant statement: 'If the devil cannot use failure to drag you down, he will use success.'[1] When feelings are running high and an air of self-reliance takes over, as it did after Jericho, then a period of self-examination is vital, because it is so easy for a church to become complacent and self-sufficient. As Arthur C. Custance once pointed out, 'The dangers to our spiritual welfare from success are far greater than the dangers from failure.'[2]

2] Israel made two major mistakes at Ai.

First of all, they trusted in their own strength rather than depending upon God's wisdom and guidance. It was not the Lord's decision to reduce the number of fighting men, as it may have been on other occasions; it was solely the decision of the men sent to spy out the country. Their advice to Joshua was flawed from the start because it was not based upon objective facts, but on an inflated view of their own capabilities. When it comes to spiritual battles, human wisdom and carnal presumption can be beguiling enemies! Soloman's pithy proverb is so apt: 'When pride comes, then comes shame; but with the humble is wisdom' (Prov. 11:2).

Israel's second serious mistake was to underestimate the strength of their enemy. The apostle Peter warns us to 'Be sober, be vigilant; because your adversary the devil walks about like a roaring lion, seeking whom he may devour' (1 Peter 5:8). We can be thankful that, as Christians, we have the authority to 'Resist him, steadfast in the faith ...' (1 Peter 5:9), and all the spiritual weapons necessary to defend ourselves from his attacks (Eph. 6:10–18). But let us never underestimate his subtlety and devious cunning. Paul could say with much discernment and experience, '... we are not ignorant of his devices' (2 Cor. 2:11). The more we are skilled in using the 'sword of the Spirit, which is the word of God' (Eph. 6:17), the more we will be enabled to resist his temptations.

3] Joshua's prayer expresses true remorse over the crushing defeat at Ai. But, alongside the deep sense of regret and guilt, he also has feelings of frustration and perplexity. Our prayers can often express a mixture of emotions and feelings which may range from fear to faith. The important thing to remember is that the Lord reads our hearts and, therefore, it is better to be open and honest before Him than to feign prayers which are meaningless and dishonest. The Psalmist is totally honest when he says, 'But as for me, my feet had almost stumbled; my steps had nearly slipped. For I was envious of the boastful, when I saw the prosperity of the wicked' (Ps. 73:2–3). Having acknowledged and confessed his temporary failure, he ends the psalm by declaring, 'But it is good for me to draw near to God ...' (Psalm 73:28). In other words, although it was painful for him to admit he had fallen, nevertheless he found it was of great benefit to be open and truthful before the One who held him by his right hand (v. 23).

4] Achan's sin had consequences, not only for him, but for all of God's people. The teaching that we are all one body in the Lord is a very comforting and encouraging truth. However, it also reminds us that each of us, as members of His body, have responsibilities to all the other members. Our attitudes and behaviour can affect the spiritual well-being of the body, either for good or ill. Paul spells out the importance of this unity in his letter to the church at Corinth. Each member, whether the 'foot' or the 'hand', has their particular place and function in the body and are not to despise or envy another member (see 1 Cor. 12:12–31).

The campaign against Ai (2)

(Joshua 8:1–29)

Setting the scene

The first attack on the city of Ai had ended in a shameful defeat for Israel because of one man's sin. However, with the death of Achan and the destruction of the 'accursed' things which he had stolen, the situation had been restored, and Joshua is commanded to 'arise' and take Ai. He is encouraged to go forward without fear or dismay in the knowledge that God has given into his hand the king and all the people of the city (v. 1). This second campaign, however, would be very different from the first debacle. The battle strategy would not originate in the minds of Joshua and his advisors but would be from the Lord (v. 2).

The attack

Joshua then, having been instructed by the Lord, sends out an ambush force at night to hide on the far side of Ai. The two elements in an ambush are concealment and surprise. Some have questioned whether the number of thirty thousand men is a correct translation of the Hebrew. The Hebrew word, elep, translated, 'thousand', can also be translated as 'captain'. If this is the case, then Joshua may have selected thirty captains as the 'mighty men of valour'—a sort of 'crack commando unit' for the dangerous task of entering the unprotected city and setting it on fire (v. 8).

The following morning, Joshua leads the main army out

toward Ai and takes up his position on the lower ground in front of the city. The same night he sends out a third detachment of five thousand men to camp between Ai and Bethel, originally called Luz (Josh. 18:13). This unit was to act as a backing force in the event of Bethel joining forces with Ai against Israel (8:12). It also served as a second ambush in the campaign to rout the forces of Ai. In all, Israel had three units of men in position: one behind the city of Ai, one to the west, and one directly in front of the city. As in the first battle, the men of Ai rushed out to attack Joshua's main unit but, this time, they feign a retreat and flee to the east. The entire army of Ai is drawn out of their city, leaving it without any protection. The unit behind Ai are given the signal by Joshua and move into action, putting the city to the torch (vv. 18–19). The smoke from the city, as it rises into the sky, alerts the army of Ai but they are now trapped and surrounded on all sides by Israel's troops, with nowhere to escape. They are all overwhelmed and struck down by Joshua's combined troops (vv. 20–22). The king of Ai is later hanged, and the inhabitants killed in obedience to God's command (v. 2).

Points for reflection

1] In the first campaign against Ai, Joshua had mistakenly leaned upon the advice of his men. They had based their calculations on a past victory, rather than looking to God for further guidance. It is as if they were saying, 'Lord, we don't need you in this battle. We can manage with just a small force of men; after all it's nothing like Jericho!' Well, there are many verses in the Bible that challenge that type of thinking. Perhaps these words in Proverbs are some of the clearest: 'Trust in the LORD with all your heart, and lean not on your own understanding; in all your ways acknowledge Him, and He shall direct your paths.' (Prov. 3:5).

2] Joshua was given a second opportunity to take the city of Ai. It is as if the first failed attempt is completely forgotten by the Lord, and He wants Joshua to press on without being plagued by regrets, or lingering doubts and fears. His command is, 'Do not be afraid, nor be dismayed ... arise, go up to Ai' (8:2). Here we see God's faithfulness to forgive and to forget His people's sins once they are acknowledged and confessed. Jonah experienced the same grace when the Word of the Lord came to Jonah 'the second time, saying, "Arise, go to Nineveh, that great city, and preach to it the message that I tell you"' (Jonah 3:1–2). Jonah's initial disobedience was followed by repentance and God sends him again, not reluctantly or hesitantly, but in grace and resolve. The same is true with Peter who, having denied the Lord, weeps bitterly and is truly repentant. His denial is not the end of his usefulness because he is wonderfully restored by Christ and commissioned to feed His sheep (John 21:17). There are always new beginnings and fresh starts in the Christian life, no matter what has gone before. Paul, writing to the Christians at Philippi, states that the one thing he does is to forget 'those things which are behind and reaching forward to those things which are ahead (Phil. 3:13). As someone has put it, 'We may fail today, but tomorrow we can triumph.'[1]

> Pardon for sin and a peace that endureth,
> Thine own dear presence to cheer and to guide;
> strength for today and bright hope for tomorrow:
> blessings all mine, with ten thousand beside!
> (Thomas O. Chisholm, 1866–1960)

Chapter 9

The Battle of Gibeon

(Joshua 10:1–27)

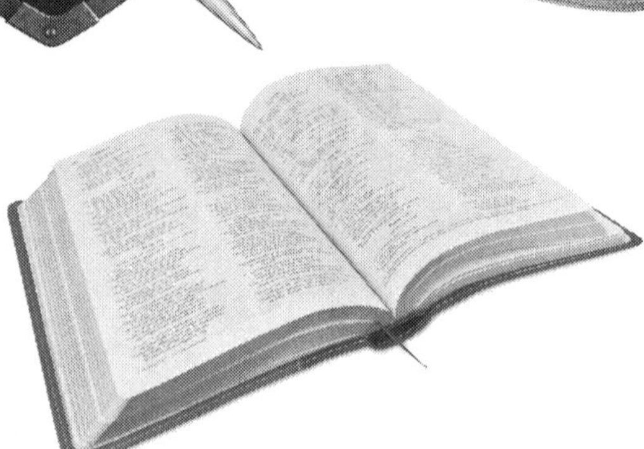

Setting the scene

This is Joshua's fourth battle in the campaign to possess the 'Promised Land' and one which deserves to be called the most 'astonishing' of all. Perhaps the key phrase in the passage recorded are the words in verse 14: 'And there has been no day like that, before it or after it, that the LORD heeded the voice of a man; for the LORD fought for Israel.'

Israel's victories against Jericho and Ai had two very different reactions among the inhabitants of Canaan. On the one hand, some of the tribes vowed to strengthen their opposition against Israel by joining together to form a military alliance (Josh. 9:1–2). On the other hand, the inhabitants of Gibeon were ready to establish a peace treaty with Israel, even if it meant an elaborate plan of deception (9:3–13). They succeeded to induce Joshua to make an alliance with them and to ensure that their lives would be spared (v. 11). This surrender was very much a 'diplomatic victory', for no blood was shed, and Gibeon, along with its neighbours, secured a peaceful settlement with Israel. But the news of this defection quickly spread to the Amorite kings and they planned to attack Gibeon, not only to punish them for their treachery, but to destroy Joshua's advance into Caanan.

This league of kings was led by Adoni-Zedik, king of Jerusalem (10:1). They laid siege to Gibeon and, immediately, its inhabitants appealed for help under the terms of their treaty with Israel (v. 6). Joshua lost no time in leaving his camp at Gilgal, some 15–20 miles from Gibeon and, under the cover of darkness, he arrived sometime before dawn, and made a surprise attack, causing confusion and panic amongst the ranks of the enemy (vv. 9–10). The word, 'routed', signifies an overwhelming and disorderly defeat, and implies terror and alarm. But the emphasis is upon the Lord's work: 'So the LORD routed them before Israel ...' (v. 10). In other words, it was the Lord who 'troubled' His enemies, as He had done against the Philistines when they were about to engulf Israel at Mizpah:

> Then Samuel cried out to the LORD for Israel, and the LORD answered him ... the Philistines drew near to battle against Israel. But the LORD thundered with a loud thunder upon the Philistines that day, and so confused them that they were overcome before Israel (1 Sam. 7:9–10).

This 'troubling' or 'discomforting' was a regular instrument of the Lord when Israel faced the threat of annihilation from their enemies.

The miraculous intervention

In their terror, the armies of the Amorites fled down the mountain pass of Beth-horon and headed down to the allied cities of Libnah, Eglon and Lachish. But there was no escape, for once again the Lord intervened to help His people and 'cast down large hailstones from heaven on them as far as Azekah, and they died' (v. 11). It was a remarkable mercy that none of the Israelite forces were injured in the torrential storm of hailstones. As someone has commented, 'God's 'ammunition fell with deadly precision.'[1] The best comment, however, comes from the Book of Job: '... have you seen the treasury of hail, which I have reserved for the time of trouble, for the day of battle and war?' (Job 38:22–23).

Yet, the miracle of the hailstorm was nothing compared with the miracle yet to come. In answer to Joshua's prayer (v. 12), God acted to give His people a complete victory by extending the hours of day light, so that Joshua's weary army could finish their task before the darkness of night could work to their enemies' advantage. Gleason L. Archer, an Old Testament scholar, interprets the phrase, 'hasted not to go down' in verse 13 (AKJV), as a 'retardation of the movement' and not a complete cessation.[2] In other words, the Lord stopped the sun and moon and then retarded the rotation of the planet so that the sun and moon set very slowly. Whichever way this miracle was achieved, we must stand in awe at God's sovereign power and care for His people. Both Joshua's bold prayer, and the answer he received, marked this particular day and battle as being unparalleled in the history of mankind: 'And there has been no day like that, before it or after it, that the LORD heeded the voice of a man; for the LORD fought for Israel' (v. 14).

The final rout

At the end of an awe-inspiring battle, Joshua concentrated on the task of retrieving the five kings who had fled for refuge and hidden themselves in a cave (vv. 16–18). He had temporarily left them there while he led his men in a 'mopping up operation' (v. 20). The few that did escape to the cities faced a further rout later (v. 40). Returning to the camp, Joshua commanded the kings to be brought before the people of Israel. The captains were ordered to put their feet upon their necks, as a symbol of conquest in the present and of future victories in the days ahead: 'Come near, put your feet on the necks of these kings. ...for thus the LORD will do to all your enemies against whom you fight' (10:24–25).

Points for reflection

1] Joshua can be seen as a picture of the Lord Jesus Christ who, as the 'Captain of our salvation' (Heb. 2:10), has defeated all His enemies, and the day is coming when He will destroy them forever (1 Cor. 15:24–28). Through Christ, we can claim the victory and put our feet on the necks of our enemies. Paul, addressing the persecuted

Christians at Rome, assures them of the coming victory: 'And the God of peace will crush Satan under your feet shortly' (Rom. 16:20).

2] Joshua's encounter with the crafty Gibeonites warns us to be discerning and cautious about making 'alliances' that can be dangerous with regard to our spiritual welfare. Paul makes this point when writing to the church at Corinth: 'Do not be deceived: "Evil company corrupts good habits"' (1 Cor. 15:33). Paul is exhorting these Christians not to keep the wrong type of company, specifically the company of those who deny the resurrection and would turn them away from the Truth. The reason given for Joshua's mistake is stated in Joshua 9:14: 'Then the men took some of their provisions; but they did not ask counsel of the Lord.' The Gibeonites' deception was well conceived and any one of us would have probably fallen for it. When the devil comes as an 'angel of light' (2 Cor. 11:14), it is very possible that we may be deceived by his craftiness. We need to be steeped in God's Word so that we can recognize the truth from the false, the good from the evil.

3] Joshua's prayer seems audaciously bold: 'Sun, stand still over Gibeon; And Moon in the Valley of Aijalon.' Yet the Lord heard him and was pleased to answer him! We, as God's children, are encouraged to 'Come boldly to the throne of grace ...' The reason for this boldness is that 'Jesus the Son of God' is also our 'great High Priest' (Heb.

4:14, 16), and He has 'purged our sins', and has 'sat down at the right hand of the Majesty on high ...' (Heb. 1:3). Paul also speaks of the boldness we have in Christ as we approach God, '... in whom we have boldness and access with confidence through faith in Him' (Eph. 3:12).

One of the many ploys of the devil is to rob us of this confidence by getting us to focus upon our sin, or upon a sense of our unworthiness in the presence of God. In Zechariah's vision, he sees 'Joshua the high priest standing before the Angel of the LORD, and Satan standing at his right hand to oppose him'. Satan stood in order to accuse the prophet of his 'filthy garments', but the Lord came to his defence by saying to those who stood before Him, '"Take away the filthy garments from him." And to [Joshua] him, He [the Lord] said, "See, I have removed your iniquity from you, and I will clothe you with rich robes"' (Zech. 3:1–4). Our confidence in the presence of God is not based upon anything in us, but solely upon the cross of Christ and His finished work, to remove our iniquity from us and to clothe us with the rich robes of His righteousness.

The Battle of Merom

(Joshua 11:1–15)

Setting the scene

In many respects the battle fought at the waters of Merom was one of the most decisive battles in Joshua's conquest of Canaan. There are two main reasons for this: firstly, the city of Hazor was the largest and most fortified city in the territory of Naphtali, with a population of over forty thousand people. Secondly, the enemy Joshua faced was both numerous and formidable: '... as many people as the sand that is on the seashore in multitude, with very many horses and chariots' (v. 4).

The coalition of kings, led by Jabin king of Hazor, converged at the gorge of Merom brook and there they set up camp in preparation to fight against Israel. This huge confederacy of armies consisted of the kings from the hill country of the north, and those also from the Arabah, south of Chinneroth (a city in Naphtali). This vast array of military power would have unnerved the best of leaders, but Joshua had been assured by the Lord that He would '... deliver all of them slain before Israel' (v. 6). In the light of this, Joshua was not to fear those massed against Israel. Joshua must have realized that a conventional encounter with all of these armies on open ground would have led to his forces being at a severe disadvantage. Not only would his foot soldiers be greatly outnumbered but they were ill equipped to confront a multi-chariot assault. The Canaanite chariots were drawn by two horses with a driver and a warrior for maximum killing power. They were very much the 'super tanks' of their day.

Joshua, therefore, opted for a surprise attack, thus seizing the initiative from the enemy and catching them off guard (v. 7). This could well have been a lightening attack at night, against a sleeping enemy—possibly an enemy that the Lord had put in a deep sleep. With their chariots destroyed by fire, and their horses disabled, they were left helpless. In the melee which followed, the Canaanites were scattered, and Joshua's forces pursued them as far as Greater Sidon in the north, and Mizpeh in the east. Joshua then turned back from the pursuit and destroyed the city of Hazor with fire. The utter destruction of Hazor was exceptional, perhaps because of its strategic position and size. Other cities that stood on 'mounds' (a heap of successive ruins) were not destroyed by fire (v. 13).

Points for reflection

1] It is important to remember that the possession and occupation of the Promised Land had to be accomplished in God's way and in God's time. Moses had outlined the principles governing Israel's warfare, some of which related to the Canaanite cities (see Deut. 20:16–17). The principle known as 'the ban of total destruction' was to be the Lord's will on this specific occasion and was faithfully adhered to by Joshua. In all respects he obeyed without hesitation or reluctance. If we, as God's people today, are faithful to the principles of our spiritual warfare, which are spelled out in the New Testament, then we can be confident that God will fight for us and enable us to triumph over our enemies (see 2 Cor. 10:4; Eph. 6:10–18).

2] Israel's clear disadvantage in military terms made no difference to the outcome of this battle. God's promise to Joshua (v. 6) was but the renewal of a promise made to the children of Israel through Moses: 'When you go out to battle against your enemies, and see horses and chariots and people more numerous than you, do not be afraid of them; for the LORD your God is with you ...' (Deut. 20:1). However disadvantaged we may feel as churches, in terms of numbers, strength or organization, we can be assured that 'He who promised is faithful,' and that '... all the promises of God in Him are Yes and in Him Amen, to the glory of God through us' (Heb. 10:23; 2 Cor. 1:20). Our greatest concern must be that God is truly among us, and that we cherish this above all else.

3] The Canaanite challenge was a challenge against God Himself. But, in reality, the contest was between God and Satan. Any attack of Satan against the Christian Church is an attack against the Lord of the Church. We may rest confidently in the knowledge that 'no weapon formed against you [us] shall prosper' (Isa. 54:17).

Against me earth and hell combine; but on my side is power divine; Jesus is all, and He is mine. Hallelujah!
(John Newton, 1725–1807)

Chapter 11

Battles during the period of judges

Ehud and the campaign against the Moabites

(Judges 3:12–30)

Setting the scene

Once again Israel's disobedience and departure from the Lord had brought them to a situation of misery and distress (v. 12). Eglon, king of Moab, leading an alliance of former enemies—the Ammonites and Amalekites—crossed the Jordan and occupied the region of Jericho ('city of palm trees', v. 13). For eighteen years Israel was reduced to serving their most bitter of enemies. At the end of that period, the people once more cried out to the Lord and He graciously heard them and gave them a deliverer: Ehud, the son of Gera, of the family of Benjamin. As in the case of Othniel, Israel's previous deliverer (Judges 3:9–11), not much is known about Ehud, apart from the fact that he shared a physical trait with many of the tribe of Benjamin—he was left-handed (v. 15).

The assassination

Ehud, determining to break the Moabite domination, conceived a plan to assassinate Eglon, and thereby create an atmosphere of confusion and uncertainty among the enemies of Israel. Leading a contingent of Israelites, he brought to Eglon a 'present' which was probably the regular tribute paid by Israel, as an admission of their subjugation to the occupying powers (v. 17). But Ehud carried under his coat a two-edged sword the size of a dagger, fastened on his right thigh (v. 16). After the delegation had dutifully presented their gift and had set off on their return journey, Ehud turned back on his own to carry out his grisly mission. Having gained an entrance into the chamber of the king who had retired to his 'summer parlour'—possibly a room situated at rooftop level with windows to catch the breeze—Ehud pretended to have a secret message for the king from God (v. 20). Eglon, curious to know what this divine oracle could be, rose up from his seat in eager anticipation. His suspicion was not aroused as Ehud used his left hand to draw the dagger from his right side, thrusting it deep into Eglon's corpulent flesh (vv. 21–22). Ehud quickly made his escape, making sure that the doors of the chamber were locked, thus delaying his crime from being detected (v. 23).

When Eglon's servants discovered that the doors of the king's chamber were locked, they assumed that he had simply responded to the call of nature (v. 24). As time passed, and suspecting something fishy, they overcame their embarrassment and came with the key to investigate. Finding their master lying dead on the floor, they must have sounded the alarm, but Ehud was well clear by this time (v. 26).

The battle against the Moabites

Arriving in the hill country of Ephraim, Ehud blew the trumpet as a call to arms and gathered an army from the men of Israel (v. 27). Confident that the Lord would now deliver His people from the Moabites, Ehud proceeded to seize the fords of the Jordan River, in order to prevent the Moabites from crossing over either to escape or receive reinforcements from their capital city of Jericho. His next move was to destroy the garrison of Moabites which numbered ten thousand men, 'all stout men of valor,' and in this he was successful (vv. 28–29). With this victory, the Moabites cruel domination over God's people was broken, and Israel was favoured with eighty years of rest from oppression and war.

Points for reflection

1] In this incident concerning Ehud and the children of Israel, we may observe two important actions of God. The first is His action against His people because of their evil ways (vv. 8, 12). But then we see what the Lord did for Israel (vv. 9, 15).

a) The Lord used Eglon to chastise His people and to bring them to their spiritual senses (v. 15). God's chastening is always meant to produce within us a greater desire to know Him, and to walk in His ways (Heb. 12:10–11). Our attitude to His chastening should, therefore, not be negative or critical, but rather positive and trustful (Heb. 12:5–6). Whenever we, as God's people, cry out to Him in faith and in humility, He hears and acts for His own glory, and for our spiritual good (2 Chr. 7:13–14).

b) In raising up Ehud, the Lord acted to deliver His people from their oppressors. He was the right man for the right time. The Lord knows when and how to help us. It may not always be the type of help we expect, but His ways are always perfect, and He sees the end from the beginning. So, we may be assured that however He acts for us, it will, without exception, be for our eternal good (Rom. 8:28).

2] As we consider Ehud's act of eliminating Eglon, there seems to be two main opinions regarding it. One views the assassination of Eglon as an outstanding act of personal heroism. Those who hold to the maxim that the 'end justifies the means', would view Ehud's deed as a necessary act against an evil tyrant. They would probably see many of Samson's solo performances against the Philistines in the same way.

A second opinion is more cautious in praising Ehud for his daring and intrepid action against Eglon. The following reasons are offered for such caution:

a) Both Ehud's two-edged sword, and his plan to murder Eglon, were of his own making (v. 16). While Scripture records the deed of Ehud in some detail, nothing is said to persuade us that it was sanctioned by God and, therefore, something that pleased Him.

b) It has been pointed out that Israel's previous deliverer, Othniel, was endowed by the 'Spirit of the LORD' (v. 10), but this is not said of Ehud.

c) The question is asked, 'Was there any need of such an act of cunning and murder to effect deliverance in Israel?'

A. E. Cundall offers the following explanation, which seems to provide a bridge between these two opinions: 'The situation had been saved by Ehud's resolution and cunning, but we are not called to admire his cold-blooded assassination of Eglon, although tyranny and oppression are themselves ugly things and are not lightly removed.'[1]

We can praise God that, in our spiritual battles, the weapons He provides are 'not carnal but mighty in God for pulling down strongholds, casting down arguments and every high thing that exalts itself against the knowledge of God' (2 Cor. 10:4–5).

Likewise, the 'two-edged sword' which we are called to use is not of our making but is indeed the Word that is of and from God (Heb. 4:12).

The Battle of Tabor

(Judges 4:1–23)

Setting the scene

The opening chapter of the book of Judges sets out to describe events after the main victories of the conquest had been gained, and when the tribes had dispersed to occupy their allocated territories. Under the leadership of Joshua, the conquest of Canaan had begun well but, with the death of Joshua, Israel failed to complete the task God had given them. The consequences of their failure would lead to faithless compromise and a cycle of backsliding, judgement and deliverance. One such judgement was the oppression and subjugation of the Canaanites by King Jabin (4:1–2). In all, God raised up twelve Judges throughout this period, but only six received special prominence: Othniel, Ehud, Deborah, Gideon, Jephthah and Samson.

It is Deborah's faith and courage which is prominent in this conflict with the Canaanite forces at Mount Tabor.

The Lord's mighty intervention

The key characters in this clash with the Canaanites were Deborah, Barak, and Jael—the daughter of Heber. Barak, whose name means 'lightening', was summoned by the prophetess, Deborah, to muster the tribes of Israel and lead them in battle against Sisera—commander of the confederate Canaanite forces. Barak managed to gather ten thousand men, mainly from the tribes of Naphtali and Zebulun, and they camped on the slopes of Mount

Tabor—a prominent mountain on the border of Zebulun in the Valley of Jezreel. The strategy was to draw Sisera's nine hundred chariots and his army to the River Kishon and the plains at the foot of Tabor. At Deborah's signal, Barak's forces swept down the slopes of Tabor, bringing panic and terror to the forces of Sisera. This crushing defeat was the result of the Lord's intervention: 'And the LORD routed Sisera and all his chariots and all his army with the edge of the sword before Barak' (4:15). In Deborah's song of triumph, we are given the exact nature of God's intervention: 'They fought from the heavens; The stars from their courses fought against Sisera. The torrent of Kishon swept them away ...' (5:20). Here, in poetic language, is described a sudden violent storm which caused the Kishon river to become a raging torrent. Both the storm and the turbulence of the swollen Kishon were God's chief instruments in Israel's victory.

The demise of Sisera

Sisera, himself, abandoned his stricken chariot and fled on foot to take refuge in the tent of Jael, the wife of Heber, an ally of Jabin, king of Canaan. Sisera, thinking he was fleeing to a place of safety, came to Jael's tent, but Jael's faithfulness to Israel had not changed, and instead of finding sanctuary and protection, he found God's justice. Jael, acting for Israel, seized the opportunity to kill the man who had ruthlessly oppressed the nation for twenty years (4:3, 21). Deborah's prophecy to Barak was dramatically fulfilled: '... for the LORD will sell Sisera into the hand of a woman' (4:9).

Points for reflection

1] We may wonder why Barak, a proven leader, was unwilling to undertake the campaign against Sisera without Deborah. If this revealed a weakness of faith, then it also reveals God's willingness to bear with our human frailty. Time and again throughout the Bible, the Lord deals patiently with His servants who are hesitant or fearful of the task assigned to them. Both Moses and Jeremiah wavered at God's call, and offered various excuses as to why they were not up to the task! (see Exod. 4:13–16; Jer. 1:6–8). Paul, writing to the Corinthians, acknowledged that his sufficiency as an apostle of Christ was from God alone (2 Cor. 3:5–6). We can praise God that He works despite our fears and falterings and gives us grace to overcome them.

2] Deborah's exhortation to Barak—'Up! For this is the day in which the LORD has delivered Sisera into your hand. Has not the LORD gone out before you?'—must have filled him with hope and confidence as he faced a daunting situation (Judg. 4:14). As we, today, face situations that may be intimidating, we can be assured that the Lord has gone before us. His ways and timing may be different from ours, but no one who trusts in the Lord will be confounded.

The promise held out by the prophet Isaiah stands today as it did when first written: 'For you shall not go out with haste, nor go by flight; For the LORD will go before you, and the God of Israel will be your rear guard' (Isa. 52:12).

3] In this incident God used unusual means to accomplish His purposes for Israel. Firstly, Deborah was the only female prophetess to judge Israel at this time. She is described as 'a mother in Israel' (Judg. 5:7), and her judicial wisdom and vibrant faith would have certainly made her an inspirational figure to all in Israel. Secondly, when we consider Sisera's demise, we may have expected him to die a warrior's death on the battlefield. But he is dispatched by a woman as he sleeps! And then, finally, what was it that brought about Sisera's defeat? A sudden cloudburst that caused a river to be flooded, which swept away the Canaanite chariotry! (Judg. 5:21). Let us be confident that, however God chooses to work in our lives, He will accomplish His eternal purposes for our good (Rom. 8:28). Wiliam Cowper's hymn seems to express this so well:

> God moves in a mysterious way,
> His wonders to perform;
> He plants His footsteps in the sea,
> And rides upon the storm.
>
> Deep in unfathomable mines
> Of never-failing skill;

He treasures up His bright designs,
And works His sovereign will.
(William Cowper, 1731–1800)

Gideon's victory over the Midianites

(Judges 7:1–25)

Setting the scene

The victorious campaign against the Midianites is the great climax in Gideon's story. It is the culmination of all the preparation and testing of this man, and it is the point at which God acted to 'save Israel from the hand of the Midianites' (Judg. 6:14).

Gideon's army of thirty-two thousand men gathered at the spring of Harod, while the army of the Midianites camped north of them in the valley near the hill of Moreh. The description of the enemy army underlines the fact that, in numerical terms, the odds were firmly stacked against Israel: 'Now the Midianites and Amalekites, all the people of the East, were lying in the valley as numerous as locusts; and their camels were without number, as the sand by the seashore in multitude' (7:12).

But then came what must have been a bewildering word from the Lord. Gideon is to reduce the number of his army because there were too many for the Lord to use to defeat the Midianites! The explanation the Lord gives for this reduction has nothing to do with military strategy. He knew that Israel would quickly claim the glory for themselves, and proudly boast, 'My own hand has saved me' (7:2).

The few separated from the many

There were two stages in the reduction of Gideon's army. Firstly, all who were afraid of fighting were given the opportunity to 'turn and depart at once from Mount Gilead' (7:3). This was one of the principles governing warfare, as outlined in Deuteronomy 20:8: 'The officers shall speak further to the people, and say, "What man is there who is fearful and fainthearted? Let him go and return to his house, lest the heart of his brethren faint like his heart."' This left ten thousand men, but again this number was far too many for the Lord's purpose, and so a further reduction was necessary.

The second stage, in the process of making Israel's fighting force even smaller, involved a test based on how the men drank water from a river or stream. A relatively small number of three hundred men used their hands to scoop up water, as a dog uses its tongue to drink. The bulk of the men, however, dropped to their knees and drank with their mouths in the water (7:4–7). The Scripture is silent as to why the three hundred men who stood to drink were chosen and, therefore, it would be better not to speculate. Suffice to say that the three hundred men were of God's choosing and not Gideon's, and that by these men the Lord would save Israel and deliver the Midianites into their hands.

Gideon receives intelligence about the enemy

The Lord orders Gideon to go down to the Midianite camp at night, with the assurance that He will give victory to Israel. However, if Gideon is afraid to attack the Midianite camp, he and his servant, Purah, are to go down, and are promised some encouragement from what they hear. As they arrived at the outposts of the enemy camp, they overhear two men discussing a dream that one of them had dreamt that night. To his alarm, the man had seen in his dream a loaf of barley bread tumbling down into their camp and knocking their tent flat to the ground. His tent-mate astonishingly interpreted the dream: 'This is nothing else but the sword of Gideon the son of Joash, a man of Israel! Into his hand God has delivered Midian and the whole camp' (7:14). With this 'divine intelligence' Gideon is moved to worship God for such a glorious revelation. On his return to the Israelite camp, he calls for them to arise because the 'Lord has delivered the camp of Midian into your hand' (v. 15).

The battle strategy

Gideon divided the three hundred men into three companies, and each man carried a trumpet in their right hand, and in the other an empty jar with a torch inside it. The plan was that Gideon, and the first hundred men, were to surround the outskirts of the camp and to blow their trumpets and break their clay jars. Then, the other two companies were to do the same, after which the three hundred men, blowing their trumpets and holding high their torches, were to shout, 'The sword of the Lord and of Gideon!' (v. 18). The result was that, as the three hundred men stood in their place around the camp, they watched as the Lord caused the Midianite soldiers, in their confusion and panic, to turn on each other with their swords. We may assume, with good reason, that the Lord Himself instilled a fear into the enemy camp since disciplined fighting men are not easily thrown into complete disarray. This was God's work!

Finally, the disarrayed army fled to places east of the Jordan (7:22). Gideon then sent for troops from neighbouring tribes to pursue the fleeing Midianites. He also sent messengers throughout the hill country of Ephraim, summoning them to come down against the Midianites and seize the fords of the River Jordan at Beth Barah, thus preventing them from making a complete escape.

Points for reflection

1] The reduction of Gideon's army presents us with some important spiritual lessons.

a) We must never glory in what we may achieve in life, whether it is success or fame or power. If we do, our hearts will quickly turn away from God. It was the Lord's grace that prevented Gideon from congratulating himself on his victory over the Midianites. The Lord knew his heart and kept him from the insidious presence of pride. Paul warned the Ephesian believers not to 'boast' in their faith in Christ, as if faith had achieved their salvation: 'For by grace you have been saved through faith, and that not of yourselves; it is the gift of God, not of works lest anyone should boast' (Eph. 2:8–9).

b] Those who were 'fearful and afraid' were allowed to return from the field of battle. Fear can be contagious, and the morale of any army is vital to its success. In the Christian life, fear can be a great stumbling-block in serving God. Paul knew that Timothy was prone to a fearful spirit and sought to address this in his letters: 'For God has not given us a spirit of fear, but of power and of love and of a sound mind' (2 Tim. 1:7). Timothy's sensitive and timid disposition was not to become something that would control him or hinder his service for Christ. Instead, he was to 'be strong in the grace that is in Christ Jesus' (2 Tim. 2:1).

c] We can imagine what was going through Gideon's mind as he saw the numbers of his army dwindling before his eyes! It is human nature to be concerned about the loss of numbers, and very often churches may consider it a sign of failure. But, in many instances, this would not be the case at all. It is of the Lord's goodness that He gave us His promise: 'For where two or three are gathered together in My name, I am there in their in the midst of them' (Matt. 18:20). While we must earnestly pray that the Lord would add to our churches 'such as should be saved', we must fight against any despondency or despair if we do not see the Lord working in this way. If He does not seem to be building His Church in our corner of the woods, we may be assured that it is being built according to His great plan and purpose elsewhere.

Conversely, we must be very careful of equating large numbers with success and divine approval! I once met a minister from Northern Ireland who told me that, although there were 1200 in his morning congregations, only a small proportion of those turned up for the mid-week prayer meeting. Surely the lesson from Gideon's experience is not to trust in numbers, but rather in the God who can work powerfully in both small and large churches.

d] God always delights to confound the wisdom of this world. It seemed so illogical to whittle Gideon's army down to 'hundreds' when they faced a foe 'as numerous as locusts' (Judges 7:12). Not only that but consider the weapons the three hundred men were to use: trumpets, empty clay jars and torches! And what about Gideon himself? In response to the Lord's call, he had exclaimed: 'O my LORD, how can I save Israel? Indeed, my clan is the weakest in Manasseh, and I am the least in my father's house' (Judg. 6:15). And then, lastly, how is he seen in the enemy's dream? Just a 'loaf of barley bread' (7:13)—a symbol of poverty and inferiority!

> Where is the wise? Where is the scribe? Where is the disputer of this age? Has not God made foolish the

wisdom of this world? ... Because the foolishness of God is wiser than men, and the weakness of God is stronger than men (1 Cor. 1:20, 25).

Abimelech's conspiracy

(Judges 9:1–56)

Setting the scene

Following the death of Gideon, Israel had, once again, reverted to a path of waywardness and unfaithfulness, turning back to the worship of Baal. As the story of Abimelech unfolds in this chapter, the consequences of Israel's defection from the Lord becomes clear. No longer are they united in their fight against their enemies, under the leadership of a man of faith, but are now intent on destroying one another, under the leadership of a man (Abimelech) who was prepared to murder his own kin. The irony of this chapter is that the main instigator of Israel's tragedy is Gideon's son, Abimelech.

Abimelech's treachery

His first treacherous act is to persuade his uncles, on his mother's side, to favour him as the successor of Gideon, rather than his seventy stepbrothers who were not of the 'family of the house of his mother's father' (9:1). He clinches their support by saying, 'Remember that I am your own flesh and bone' (9:2). When his uncles go to the men of Shechem to discuss Abimelech's scheme, they see no reason why their 'brother' should not be supported and give him money from the temple offerings of the idol Baal-Berith (v. 4). With the money he hires a bunch of 'worthless and reckless men' and, together, they set off to slaughter all of Abimelech's half-brothers (v. 5). But

Jotham, the youngest brother, escapes and finds a secure hideout.

The full extent of Abimelech's atrocity reaches the ears of Jotham who shouts to the men of Shechem from the top of Mount Gerizim. His parable about the trees wanting a king, and the application of it to the men of Shechem, is a masterpiece of reasoning and sound judgment (9:7–15)! As someone has wisely said, 'The point of the parable is that they had selected the wrong person to rule over them.'[1]

Abimelech's downfall

After Abimelech had ruled over Israel for three years as a self-styled hero, the men of Shechem turned against him. An evil spirit sent by God stirs them up to resent his leadership; they also hate him for the crime against his brothers and want him to be punished for it (vv. 22–24). A second selfish opportunist, named Gaal, enters the scene. Seeing an advantage to empower himself because of the disaffection in Shechem, he persuades various bands of villains in the city to make him their leader. Very soon, Abimelech is despised by the men of Shechem and seen as a spent force. Zebul, who is Abimelech's deputy, hears of Gaal's treachery and warns Abimelech to make preparations for a night-time ambush against Gaal (vv. 30–33). Abimelech listens to his advice and employs his forces into four companies outside the city of Shechem. The following morning, Gaal spots a movement of men advancing toward the city. He immediately exclaims to Zebul, 'Look, people are coming down from the tops of the mountain!' But Zebul tries to lull Gaal into thinking that his eyes are playing tricks on him, and that what he really sees are the shadows of the mountains (v. 36). But Gaal is unconvinced and with greater certainty describes the scene: 'See, people are coming down from the center of the land, and another company is coming from the Diviner's Terebinth tree' (v. 37). Cunningly, Zebul changes his tune and challenges Gaal to live up to what he has boasted with his mouth concerning Abimelech. So Gaal engages in battle with the troops of Abimelech and is defeated, and many are wounded and flee back to the city. Zebul, who has his own forces drives them out of Shechem (vv. 38–40).

Abimelech, however, is not content to leave the matter there. He plans to take his revenge on the people of Shechem for their rebellion. As they return to their normal work in the fields, he sends his men to kill them and to completely destroy the city of Shechem. When all the people of the tower of Shechem hear of this massacre they seek refuge in the stronghold of the temple of the idol, Berith, but they too perish as Abimelech sets fire to the building. He next attacks the neighbouring city of Thebez, which may have supported Shechem in their uprising.

Again, the people of Thebez seek shelter in their strong tower. But, as Abimelech and his forces draws close to the tower to do as they did in Shechem, a woman (unnamed) saves the day by dropping a millstone on Abimelech's head, causing severe damage to his skull. In a pathetic effort to save his reputation, he calls for his armour bearer saying, 'Draw your sword and kill me, lest men say of me, "A woman killed him"' (vv. 42–55).

Points for reflection

If ever the words of Moses to the children of Israel were clearly illustrated, it is surely in the story of Abimelech: '... Take note, you have sinned against the Lord; and be sure your sin will find you out' (Num. 32:23).

We can trace a number of sinful incidents which had serious consequences for the various participants involved:

1] Firstly, there is the sin of Gideon in associating with a woman from Shechem, and having a son by her, whose name was Abimelech. As we have seen, this had far-reaching consequences for all his family, and for the people of Israel (Judg. 8:31). One of the reasons why God hates sin is that it is so destructive in its effects upon mankind. Individuals, and nations alike, are destroyed by sin, whether it is in terms of relationships, health, or governance. What we all need to realize is that sin does have its consequences, even though we thank God that the penalty for sin has been paid for, once and for all, in the death of the Lord Jesus Christ.

> The terrors of law and of God
> with me can have nothing to do;
> my Saviour's obedience and blood
> hide all my transgressions from view.
> (Augustus Montague Toplady, 1740–78)

2] Secondly, there is the sin of the men of Shechem, in aiding and abetting Abimelech to kill all his half-brothers (9:57). Jotham's words to the men of Shechem: '... let fire come out of the bramble [Abimelech] and devour the cedars of Lebanon [the men of Shechem]', finally caught up with them, because they had not 'acted in truth and sincerity' (9:16, 19), concerning Gideon and his family.

3] Thirdly, there is the sin of Abimelech. We can point to at least three things which contributed to his downfall:

a) To begin with we must mention his pride. Abimelech's name means, 'My father was king', but Gideon, his father, had refused kingship and had refused it for his son (Judg. 8:22–23). But Abimelech went to great lengths of evil and force to achieve his ambition to rule over Israel. Augustine famously said, 'Pride is the perverse desire of height.'[2] Things may have been very different if Abimelech took to heart his father's conviction that the Lord was the true King over the children of Israel: '... the LORD shall rule over you'. Sadly, it is not unusual in the Bible for godly fathers to produce ungodly sons.

b) Then we see the sin of vengeance. This is manifested in two main ways:

- Firstly, Abimelech's ruthless desire to eliminate his half-brothers, who he viewed as being in a more favourable position than himself—thus being a threat to his ambition and plans. As the son of a concubine from Shechem, and not the son of a true Israelite, this would have produced within him a sense of inferiority. We are not given any details with regard to his relationship with the seventy other sons of Gideon, but the wholesale slaughter of these men showed that his heart was filled with hatred and contempt for them all.
- The second manifestation of the sin of vengeance is seen in the way Abimelech reacted to those who had become disloyal and had followed the upstart, Gaal. His desire for revenge and retribution led to a conflict which resulted in his death at the hands of an unknown woman. The tragedy of pride and unbelief is that it always leads to death. The Pharisees, who continued to show pompous unbelief towards Jesus, were told that they would die in their sins (John 8:24).

The Bible makes it clear that vengeance must have no part in the life of the Christian. It is something which is to be left entirely with God: '"Vengeance is Mine, I will repay," says the Lord' (Heb. 10:30).

Thomas Brooks wonderfully defines envy, which so often leads to a vengeful spirit:

> Envy, it tortures the affections, it vexes the mind, it inflames the blood, it corrupts the heart, it wastes the spirits; and so it becomes man's tormentor and man's executioner at once.[3]

As we ponder Brook's erudite analysis of the harm of harbouring feelings of resentment and jealousy, we see how important it is to leave vengeance to a holy and righteous God, for He alone will deal justly with those who may 'revile and persecute you, and say all kinds of evil against you falsely for My sake' (Matt. 5:11). Our calling as Christians is to resist the temptation to avenge ourselves, or to follow our natural instinct to retaliate. We praise God that we are no longer ruled by our natural instincts, but rather by the leading and power of the Holy Spirit.

> Therefore, brethren, we are debtors—not to the flesh, to live according to the flesh. ... For as many as are led by the Spirit of God, these are sons of God (Rom. 8:12, 14).

Jephthah's victory over of the Ammonites

(Judges 11:1–33)

Setting the scene

Along with Gideon, Barak and Samson, the hero of this chapter is included in Hebrews Chapter 11 as a man who lived and died by faith. But, as was true of his fellow Judges, Jephthah's character was less than straightforward, and revealed inconsistencies in wisdom and judgement. It is as if the Bible is constantly asking the question, 'What hero or heroine of faith is not blighted in some way by sin?' The answer, of course, is none! Only the Lord Jesus Christ is 'holy, harmless, undefiled, separate from sinners' (Heb. 7:26).

Jephthah's start in life was not the best of beginnings. Born the son of a prostitute and considered as a pariah by his stepbrothers, Jephthah suffered the humiliation of being driven out by his family (v. 2). This event had a profound impact upon him and, to a large extent, determined the whole course of his future life. He came to live in a place called Tob, a region south of Damascus, and soon attracted other outcasts and social misfits who gathered around him. As their leader, he organized raids into areas opposed to Israel, thus becoming a sort of Robin Hood character. In spite of Jephthah's dire misfortune, he possessed a dignity and a faith which singled him out from his contemporaries: he was 'a mighty man of valour' (a courageous warrior) (v. 1).

The opportunity arose for Jephthah to show his

'valour'. It came when Israel was threatened with invasion from the people of Ammon, who lived in the territory east of the Jordan. Fearing the worst of outcomes from their enemy, the elders of Gilead realized their desperate need of Jephthah's warrior skills and set off to find him at Tob (v. 5). Jephthah did not immediately agree to their request, but reminded them of their past hatred towards him, and their callous treatment in sending him away (v. 7). But then, having made his expectations known to them, he is given an assurance by the elders of Gilead that they will make him the head and commander over them, and Jephthah accedes to their requests (v. 11).

Jephthah becomes the commander of Israel.

As the recognized leader of God's people, Jephthah's initial response to the aggression of Ammon is a diplomatic one. He seeks an explanation from Ammon for their desire for war, and their violation of his territory (v. 12). Their counter claim is that the land belongs to them, but it was stolen from them by Israel. What follows is Jephthah's detailed defence of Israel's claim to the land.

He makes three important points:

a] Firstly, he argues that Israel behaved with restraint and courtesy when faced with a refusal to allow them passage through the land of Edom and Moab, on their journey to Canaan. The same thing happened when Israel requested access through King Sihon's territory. Not only did Sihon refuse, but he attacked the people of Israel. However, the Lord gave them victory over Sihon, and they gained a rightful possession of the land (vv. 14–22).

b] Secondly, Jephthah makes it clear that it was 'the Lord God of Israel' who dispossessed the Amorites and therefore Israel, being the people of God, received the land as a gift from Him (v. 23).

c] Thirdly, Jephthah argues that Israel had dwelt in the land for three hundred years, and yet no attempt by the Amorites had been made during that long period of time to recover the land that they claimed to own (v. 26).

Sadly, Jephthah's diplomacy failed. Israel's enemy was bent on war (v. 28).

Jephthah's vow and victory over Ammon

As in the case of Gideon and Samson, the Spirit of the Lord empowered Jephthah for the task He had assigned him (v. 29; see also 6:34 and 14:19). In this renewed strength Jephthah travelled north, recruiting men from the tribes of Gad and Manasseh (v. 29). The victory over Ammon is somewhat overshadowed by Jephthah's rash promise to God. He vowed to sacrifice a human life (not the life of an animal) if the Lord delivered Ammon into his hands. Human sacrifice was completely forbidden by the Mosaic law (Lev. 18:21; Deut. 12:31). Jephthah may not have planned to sacrifice his daughter, but he should have known that God's favour could not be gained by such a terrible act. Sadly, both his vow and his victory turned out to be a very costly one. We cannot be absolutely certain whether Jephthah's daughter suffered a lifetime of perpetual virginity or was indeed a victim of human sacrifice (v. 39).

Points for reflection

1] The book of Ecclesiastes gives us some good advice with regard to making promises to God: 'Do not be rash with your mouth, and let not your heart utter anything hastily before God. For God is in heaven, and you on earth; Therefore let your words be few' (Eccles. 5:2). Another cautionary note is struck in the book of Deuteronomy:

> When you make a vow to the LORD your God, you shall not delay to pay it; for the LORD your God will surely require it of you, and it would be sin to you. ... That which has gone from your lips you shall keep and perform, for you voluntarily vowed to the LORD your God what you have promised with your mouth (Deut. 23:21, 23).

A few practical points are made in these two passages. To begin with, any promise made to God needs to be thought about carefully, and if we think we cannot keep it, it is best not to make it in the first place. Then secondly, the Lord does not require us to make promises to Him, but He does require us to obey Him. And thirdly, although we are free not to make vows to Him, any promise we do make ought to be kept.

2] Jephthah began life with a double handicap which was not of his own making. Being born of a prostitute, he was an illegitimate son and, therefore, at a great disadvantage as far as his social and family status was concerned. But in spite of this, the Lord was pleased to use him in a most remarkable way. How wonderful to know that our position in our family, or our standing in society, is never something that prevents us from being used in God's service. When Samuel saw Eliab, the eldest son of Jesse, he was really impressed by his physique and immediately thought that he was God's choice to be the next king. But this is what the Lord said to him: 'Do not look at his appearance or at his physical stature ... for man looks at the outward appearance, but the LORD looks at the heart' (1 Sam. 16:7). The Lord is concerned with what we are on the inside, rather than what we may appear to be on the outside.

3] Jephthah's rise to eminence and power came as a result of God's calling rather than human manipulation and maneuvering. The Psalmist reveals the fallacy of 'self-promotion' or the idea that elevation of any kind is in the hands of man alone: 'For exaltation comes neither from the east nor from the west nor from the south. But God is the Judge: He puts down one, and exalts another' (Ps. 75:6, 7).

Samson's victory over the Philistines

(Judges 15:9–15)

Setting the scene

Although Samson's conflict with the Philistines can hardly be classed as a conventional battle, yet it has important lessons for us as God's people today. Samson, like Jephthah, had contradictory elements in his character. As a judge in Israel, it has to be said that he fulfilled his calling in rather unorthodox ways and it was only God's grace that turned some of his failings into successes. Sadly, his life-story centered around his problematic relationships with Philistine women. 'By treating his Nazirite vows loosely, ... Samson was careless about honouring God at all times.'[1]

Some have even sought to question Samson's role, altogether, as a deliverer of Israel, but that would be to question the sovereign providence of God. He was raised up for a particular time and a particular task, and that seems to be the key to understanding Samson's place in Israel's history. The time of the Judges was a dark and turbulent time for Israel but, sadly, this unrest was of their own making, as is clear from the description of their terrible backsliding, stated in Judges 10:6–8:

> Then the children of Israel again did evil in the sight of the LORD, and served the Baals and the Ashtoreths, the gods of Syria, the gods of Sidon, the gods of Moab, the gods of the people of Ammon, and the gods of the Philistines; and they forsook

> the LORD and did not serve Him. So the anger of the LORD was hot against Israel; and He sold them into the hands of the Philistines and into the hands of the people of Ammon. From that year they harassed and oppressed the children of Israel for eighteen years ...

So, at the time of Samson's adulthood, the children of Israel, under the yoke of the Philistines, had sunk into a spiritual apathy and paralysis. The men of Judah had completely capitulated to their oppressors and were, therefore, unable to form any kind of army to resist the subjugation of their enemies. Samson's 'one man' enterprises, which were so wonderfully used of God, are, therefore, to be seen in this light.

Samson's single-handed victory over the Philistines

Samson's battle against the thousand Philistines followed two humiliating events in his life. The first was Samson's failed attempt to be reconciled to his wife. Taking a young goat as a kind of peace offering, Samson requested an opportunity to enter into his wife's room. His father-in-law, however, did not allow him to see his wife, stating that he had really thought that Samson hated her and, for this reason, had given her to one of Samson's companions (Judg. 15:1–2). The second humiliation came when Samson was rejected and betrayed by the men of

Judah. They were scornful at his revenge against the Philistines, who had cruelly killed his wife and father-in-law by burning them alive as a punishment for Samson's attack on their fields of grain (Judg. 15:3–6, 11). Instead of fighting with Samson against their common enemy, they opted to hand Samson over to the Philistines, hoping to secure a peace which, in turn, would result in them being left alone by the Philistines. Tying him with strong ropes, they brought him to Lehi, where the Philistines came 'shouting' to meet him. But, at that point, the Spirit of the Lord came mightily upon him, enabling him to snap the ropes as if they were burnt pieces of flax. Seizing a fresh jawbone of a donkey, Samson struck and killed a thousand men. He called that place of victory, Ramath Lehi (meaning 'Jawbone Height') (Judg. 15:16–17):

> With the jawbone of a donkey, Heaps upon heaps,
> With the jawbone of a donkey I have slain a thousand men!

Points for reflection

1] Samson's story is a story of great contrasts and contradictions. There is the element of remarkable physical strength, but also of lamentable moral weakness. There is the presence of spiritual faithfulness, but there are also the occasions of serious lapses of disobedience. While it is true that many of Samson's actions were the result of a complex personality, the lack of a consistent faith and a desire to please the Lord contributed to his erratic behaviour. But it is not without significance that Samson takes his place with those men and women '... who through faith ... worked righteousness, obtained promises ... became valiant in battle, turned to flight the armies of the aliens' (Heb. 11:33–34). This surely is a testimony to the truthful and gracious content of the Scriptures!

As believers we should strive to be consistent in our Christian lives. Paul exhorts the believers at Thessalonica to 'hold fast to what is good' and to 'abstain from every form of evil'. Both positive and negative aspects of Paul's teaching are vital if we are to maintain a balanced consistency in our walk with God (1 Thes. 5:21–22). It is a cause of great wonder and praise that Jesus our Saviour was perfectly consistent in His obedience and love for His Father, thus gaining a righteousness for us that we could never had attained for ourselves.

2] Samson found himself rejected by his wife and by his own people. This rebuff, from the very people he had been appointed to deliver, must have caused him much pain and anguish. Yet this rejection is but a pale reflection of the suffering of the One sent to be our Deliverer: 'He was in the world ... and the world did not know Him. He came to His own, and His own did not receive Him' (John 1:10–11). It was not only the world of men that rejected Christ but, because He became our sin bearer, God the Father turned from His beloved Son. His cry from the cross, 'My God, My God, why have You forsaken Me' (Matt. 27:46), signifies the agony of being the object of the Father's wrath, and the utter anguish of being 'stricken' and 'smitten' by God for our transgressions (Isa. 53:4).

As Christians, we may well be rejected by the world because of our trust in the Lord Jesus Christ. While such rejection might be hurtful, the truth is that, once we are in Christ, we will never know what it is to be rejected by God and such a truth ought to fill us with thankfulness and joy.

> The soul that on Jesus hath leaned for repose,
> I will not, I will not desert to its foes,
> That soul, though all hell should endeavor to shake,
> I'll never, no never, no never forsake.'
> ('K' in Rippon's SELECTION of Hymns, 1787.)

3] While we may almost gasp at Samson's spirit of revenge, and his yearning to retaliate against those who had wronged him, we must remember that he was not acting only in a personal capacity. He was God's instrument for judging the Philistines. This one man became, in God's hands, more powerful than the whole nation! Yet, it is also true to say that Samson's personal vengeance brought him much trouble and great unhappiness. Our Lord's teaching on personal revenge and retaliation is very clear:

> You have heard that it was said, 'An eye for an eye and a tooth for a tooth.' But I tell you not to resist

> an evil person. But whoever slaps you on your right cheek, turn the other to him also. If anyone wants to sue you and take away your tunic, let him have your cloak also. And whoever compels you to go one mile, go with him two. Give to him who asks you, and from him who wants to borrow from you do not turn away (Matt. 5:38–42).

This, surely, is the way of true blessedness.

Chapter 17

Battles during the United Kingdom/ Divided Period

The Ark of God captured

(1 Samuel 4:2–11)

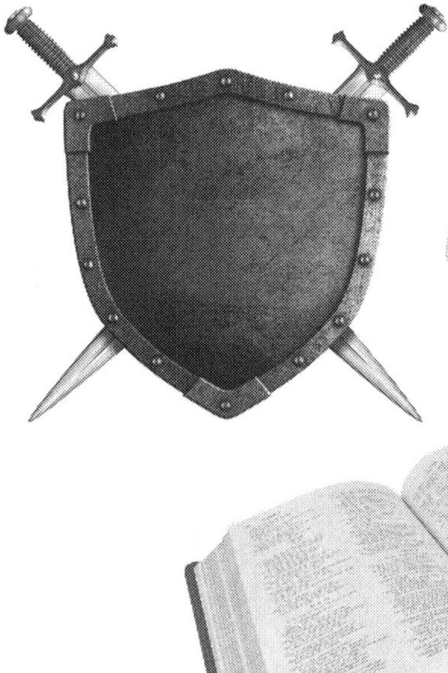

Setting the scene

This chapter records one of the most disastrous events in Israel's early history. The doleful question of the elders of Israel, when the people returned to the camp after fighting the Philistines was this: 'Why has the LORD defeated us today before the Philistines?' (v. 3). It had its answer in Israel's flagrant disobedience and unfaithfulness, which was characterized by the corrupt conduct of Eli's two sons, Hophni and Phinehas (see 1 Sam. 2:12–17). The seriousness of their unscrupulous behaviour as the 'priests of the LORD' is described in verse 17 of 1 Samuel 2: 'Therefore the sin of the young men was very great before the LORD, for men abhorred the offering of the Lord.'

Israel's ignorance and superstition

The two battles fought against the Philistines, both of which ended in humiliating defeats, can be traced to Israel's estrangement from God, and their unwillingness to act upon His Word. Certain things stand out as grave misjudgments by the people of Israel.

The first was their call for the ark of the covenant to be brought from its place in the sanctuary at Shiloh. It seems clear that the people understood their defeat was more to do with the Lord withdrawing His favour and help, than the military power of the Philistines. In a vain effort to secure the Lord's presence with them, they sent for the object which they believed would guarantee their victory (vv. 3–4). The ark, as a sacred symbol of God's glory and manifested presence, was used in this instance as an object of superstition, which only revealed their ignorance and fear.

Then secondly, when the ark finally reached the camp of Israel, we read that '... all Israel shouted so loudly that the earth shook' (v. 5). If this shout was made with the hope of the Philistines losing any will to fight against them, it was, as later proved, a false hope. Their shout also betrayed an ill-judged confidence. The glory of Israel was Israel's God, not the ark itself.

But thirdly, Israel's false hope and confidence culminated in a false expectation. Instead of the triumph they had expected, the outcome was very different. The Philistines resolved to overcome their trepidation of the ark of the covenant, and fought with great tenacity, driving the Israelites from the battlefield, and capturing the ark of God (vv. 9–11).

Points for reflection

1] The world today is full of people who have false hopes, which are based on ignorance and superstition. Only recently, I watched an interview on a well-known video-sharing platform which underlined the confusion and blindness that people have about what happens to them when they die. A woman was describing her 'after death' experience. She explained how she had entered a different realm and felt completely free as she floated about in light. She claimed that she was no longer afraid of death and now could look forward to living a life regardless of what people thought of her. There was no mention of Christ or of being aware of God's presence. She had not talked about faith in Jesus or the gift of salvation. Indeed, there was nothing at all which corresponded to the truth of the Bible. She received of course, enthusiastic applause from the studio audience, and praise from her interviewer.

Sadly, many people entertain false hopes about what will happen to them when they die. The Scriptures are the only authority on this crucial subject. The writer to the Hebrews states that '... it is appointed for men to die once, but after this the judgement' (Heb. 9:27). Our hope, as Christians, is not based upon some imagined experience of heaven, but upon the facts of the gospel, as summarized by the apostle Paul:

> For I delivered to you first of all that which I also received: that Christ died for our sins according to the Scriptures, and that He was buried, and that He rose again the third day according to the Scriptures ... (1 Cor. 15:3–4).

2] This incident also has lessons for us as the people of God. The Church, too, can entertain various false hopes. If Christians put their trust in a particular denomination, or in a popular preacher, or in a particular style of worship, and think of these things as guaranteeing some sort of divine favour or blessing, they are just as misguided as the children of Israel. Our trust must be in God alone.

3] Israel's failure to answer their own question, in v. 3, resulted in their unwarranted confidence. If the elders had sat down and really given thought to 'why' the Lord had not given them the victory over the Philistines, they would have been more reluctant to fight a second battle! As one godly teacher has put it, 'If they had said, "Let us think," instead of, "Let us act," then perhaps they would have been able to answer their own question.'[1]

Again, this can be true of us today. Sometimes we are too quick to act, too quick to find solutions, and too quick to put our confidence in our own solutions! There is, of course, a time for action but we are never to abandon the use of our minds. Thinking through a problem and praying about a problem can be seen as complementary activities and both have their place in the Christian life.

4] False hopes and a false confidence inevitably lead to false expectations. It is not wrong to have 'great expectations', as long as those expectations are founded on a true hope and a true confidence in God.

> Our God, our help in ages past,
> Our hope for years to come,

Our shelter from the stormy blast
And our eternal home.
(Isaac Watts, 1674–1748)

Saul's battle against Ammon

(1 Samuel 11:1–11)

Setting the scene

This was Saul's first battle and, as such, it established him as the future leader and king of Israel. There were some who had questioned Saul's ability to rule over the nation, but this resounding victory over the Ammonite forces vindicated Saul in the eyes of the people and they were now eager to welcome him as their king (v. 12).

We know, however, that what seemed to start so well, ended in failure and decline, and in Saul being rejected as Israel's king. It soon became clear that Saul's attitude and actions betrayed a disregard for God's Word. This is made plain in Samuel's rebuke, when Saul had taken things into his own hands and acted without any priestly authority:

> And Samuel said to Saul, 'You have done foolishly. You have not kept the commandment of the LORD your God, which He commanded you. For now the LORD would have established your kingdom over Israel forever. But now your kingdom shall not continue' (1 Sam. 13:13–14).

The Lord's words to Samuel, later, only confirmed what Samuel had predicted would happen to Saul: 'Now the word of the LORD came to Samuel, saying, "I greatly regret that I have set up Saul as king, for he has turned back from following Me, and has not performed My commandments"' (1 Sam. 15:10).

Saul defends the people of Jabesh Gilead

When the children of Israel entered the Land of Promise they were kept from attacking the people of Ammon. The Lord commanded Moses 'not to harass them or meddle with them', because they were regarded as relatives of the Israelites (Deut. 2:19). But, in the period of the Judges, Ammon aided Eglon in subduing Israel (Judg. 3:13). They now threatened the Israelite town of Jabesh Gilead by besieging it.

The men of the town approached Nahash, the Ammonite king, and asked if they could agree a peace treaty with them. His condition for such a treaty was particularly cruel and gruesome: 'On this condition I will make a covenant with you, that I may put out all your right eyes, and bring reproach on all Israel' (1 Sam. 11: 2). Their response to this was to ask for time, so that they could send messengers throughout Israel and plead for help.

When they came to Saul's hometown, they reported the dire situation to the people, who immediately wept aloud (v. 4). When Saul inquired about the sight of them weeping, the Spirit of God came upon him and moved him into action. He divided a pair of oxen and sent the pieces throughout all the land of Israel, with this warning: 'Whoever does not go out with Saul and Samuel to battle, so it shall be done to his oxen' (v. 7). Under the fear of the Lord, the people rallied around Saul and a substantial army was formed in order to save Jabesh Gilead.

Saul's battle tactics

The stratagem Saul employed to engage in battle with Nahash, had been tried and tested by leaders such as Gideon and Abimelech. He divided his army into three companies, with the intention of surrounding the enemy, and launched an attack during the early hours of the morning, probably as the enemy slept (v. 11a). It was a complete rout, with most of the Ammonites killed by midday. The rest of the enemy were so badly scattered that no two of them were left together (v. 11b). Saul was quick to give God the glory for this victory: '... today the LORD has accomplished salvation in Israel' (v. 13).

Points for reflection

1] When we think of Saul himself, he is something of a conundrum. Was he a true believer, or did he use religion for his own advantage? There seems to be evidence to prove that both of these were true of him!

We have, first of all, the words of Samuel to Saul: '... the Spirit of the LORD will come upon you, and you will ... be turned into another man' (1 Sam. 10:6). Then in verse 9 of the same chapter: 'So it was, when he had turned his back to go from Samuel, that God gave him another heart'.

From what we read of his early reign, a genuine change had taken place.

But some would question the depth of this change and argue that the major part of Saul's life revealed only his waywardness and self-interest. Perhaps the greatest sadness about Saul's life was that he failed to appreciate the many privileges he was favoured with. He was blessed by having Samuel as his spiritual guide and friend. He was granted the opportunity of having David's presence with him when he became agitated and distressed. His son, Jonathan, was an example of godliness and courage, and remained faithful to him throughout his life. He was hailed as a great military leader and then, of course, he was exalted and honoured as Israel's first king. Yet sadly, these and many other privileges were squandered because of his stubborn and willful actions—which in the end were the ruin of him.

How we need to be thankful for the spiritual privileges God has bestowed on us and pray that we might make use of them for His glory and praise. Are we now living at a time when we are free to worship God, free to hear the Word of God preached, free to share our testimony of God's saving grace with others? Yes, we are, but the time may come, sooner than we may expect, when these freedoms and privileges will no longer be ours.

2] By choosing the battle tactics which had been tried and tested by military leaders in the past, Saul was following a path of wisdom. Likewise, today, if the Church is to know success and victory in its battles against the world, the flesh and the devil, it must walk in the old paths:

> Thus says the LORD: 'Stand in the ways and see, and ask for the old paths, where the good way is, and walk in it; then you will find rest for your souls' (Jer. 6:16).

There is no substitute for the faithful preaching of God's Word, for earnest and heartfelt prayer, and for a wholehearted desire for holiness. These alone will bring rest to our souls and enable us to triumph over our enemies.

3] In contrast to Saul's wisdom, we see Nahash's foolishness. He was so confident of crushing Jabesh Gilead, that he gave them the opportunity to seek the help of all the territories of Israel. He probably estimated that Israel was both too weak and unwilling to help them, but he overlooked a supremely important fact. The nation of Israel was God's army, and He was the leader of His people in its battles:

> And it came to pass at the end of the four hundred and thirty years—on that very same day—it came to pass that all the armies of the LORD went out from the land of Egypt (Exod. 12:41).

> And Moses said to the people, 'Do not be afraid. Stand still, and see the salvation of the LORD, which

> He will accomplish for you today. ... The LORD will fight for you, and you shall hold your peace' (Exod. 14:13–14).

The Church today may face many battles, both with seen and unseen enemies, but those who foolishly rage against her will always suffer defeat, because the Lord is always 'mighty in battle' (Ps. 24:8).

> Fierce may be the conflict,
> Strong may be the foe,
> But the King's own army
> None can overthrow;
> Round His standard ranging,
> Victory is secure,
> For His truth unchanging
> Makes the triumph sure.
> (Frances Ridley Havergal, 1836–79)

Chapter 19

David and Goliath

(1 Samuel 17: 1–58)

Setting the scene

David's first appearance on the battlefield was not as a soldier in the army of Israel, but as an errand boy for his elderly father, Jesse. His mission was to take a supply of food for his three older brothers, who had joined the forces of Saul to fight against the Philistines at the Valley of Elah. Jesse's other purpose, in sending David to the battleground, was to report on his three sons and to bring him news of their welfare (vv. 17–18).

David arrives at the camp

Having reached the encampment of Israel, David deposited his provisions with the supply keeper and hurried to the front ranks to speak with his brothers. No sooner had he greeted them than the Philistine champion, Goliath of Gath, appeared as before, with menacing and threatening words of defiance, terrifying the men of Israel (17:10, 23). The news that had circulated throughout the camp, that Saul would give his daughter to the man who killed Goliath, had reached the ears of David and his reaction was one of righteous disdain for the Philistine: 'For who is this uncircumcised Philistine, that he should defy the armies of the living God?'(v. 26).

The immediate response from his oldest brother, Eliab, was one of scorn and complaint, accusing him of dereliction of duty in leaving his sheep, only to pry into things that did not concern him (v. 28). But, disregarding his brother's censure, he went on to speak to others in the ranks, and finally found himself before the king, saying confidently, 'Let no man's heart fail because of him; your servant will go and fight with this Philistine' (v. 32).

Saul's initial response was to call into question David's youth and lack of military experience. However, David explained how he had fought both lion and bear to protect his sheep and the Lord, who had delivered him on those occasions, would deliver him from 'this uncircumcised Philistine' (vv. 33–37). Saul, greatly impressed with David's spunk and faith, dressed him in his own armour, but the armour only served to hinder David's movement, so it was quickly discarded (vv. 38–40).

David advances toward Goliath

Taking only his staff, sling and a handful of chosen stones from a stream, David moved closer to his fierce opponent. The giant's tirade of contempt for David, uttered with the intention of both intimidating and petrifying him (vv. 43–44), was met by a glorious oration of David's trust and confidence in the Lord:

> I come to you in the name of the LORD of hosts, the God of the armies of Israel, whom you have defied. This day the LORD will deliver you into my hand … that all the earth may know that there is a God in Israel (vv. 45–46).

With his bold reliance upon God, David positioned himself to strike Goliath with his sling. The stone found its target and the giant fell helplessly to the ground. Then, using Goliath's own sword, David severed his head, making sure that life was no longer in the enemy of God and His people (vv. 48–51). With their champion dead, the Philistines fled in disarray, only to be pursued by the men of Israel and Judah who overwhelmed them on the way to Gath and Ekron. After plundering their camp, the Israelites returned to Jerusalem and David himself also returned, bringing with him the head of the Philistine. Abner, the commander of the army, brought David before Saul, whose question to David was loaded with both curiosity and admiration: 'Whose son are you, young man?' to which David replied, 'I am the son of your servant Jesse the Bethlehemite' (vv. 57, 58) This would be the start of a long and complex relationship between David and Saul, ending in Saul's tragic defeat and death during a battle against the Philistines at Mount Gilboa.

Points for reflection

1] David's righteous indignation, on hearing the blasphemous and arrogant taunts of Goliath, reveals how deeply he regarded the honour and glory of God. This concern for God's name issued in the brave action he took to deliver Israel from their paralyzing fear. A similar concern gripped the apostle Paul's heart as he waited for Silas and Timothy at Athens. Luke tells us that Paul's 'spirit was provoked within him when he saw that the city was given over to idols' (Acts 17:16). This led Paul to address the Athenians about their superstition and ignorance, and to proclaim to them the 'Lord of heaven and earth' who 'commands all men everywhere to repent' (Acts 17:24, 30). Are our hearts stirred within us when we see and hear how people ignorantly dismiss the truth of the gospel, and does this lead us to pray and actively seek that God's glory will be seen in the salvation of men and women?

2] In this incident we see how David overcame a number of possible discouragements, which could have shaken his resolve to fight against Goliath:

a) Firstly, we must start with his present circumstances, which were unsettling and unresolved. It was not only a period of transition and change in his life, but also a period of uncertainty. He had been anointed by Samuel to be the future king of Israel but had no idea when and how this would take place (1 Sam. 16:13). In addition to this, he was spending some time in Saul's court, and the rest of his time he was tending the sheep at Bethlehem. Nothing seemed settled. Yet, for all these unresolved circumstances, David seemed unshakable in his faithfulness to God. Many years later he wrote these lovely words: 'Rest in the LORD and wait patiently for Him' (Psalm 37:7). There may be many situations in our own lives which can be unsettling, causing us to feel disturbed and anxious about the future. At such times the only true antidote is to heed Christ's invitation to rest in His grace:

> Come to Me, all you who labour and are heavy laden, and I will give you rest. Take My yoke upon you and learn from Me, for I am gentle and lowly in heart, and you will find rest for your souls. For My yoke is easy and My burden is light (Matt. 11: 28–30).

b) Then there is Goliath himself. There could hardly have been a greater contrast between the youthful David, with his simple sling, and the giant of Gath, with his panoply of armour and weapons! Not only this of course, but there was his sheer size towering above David, measuring over 9 feet tall (approx. 2.7 metres). Furthermore, this man was not a quiet giant! No, his voice bellowed across the valley, threatening to feed David's flesh to the birds and to the wild animals! Both the sight and sound of this man was enough to terrify the whole army of Israel. But David stood firm, and was not intimidated by all his violent threats and his menacing appearance. What then, was David's secret? The answer is in the way he viewed God, which seemed to be so different from everyone around him. His eyes were not locked on Goliath, but rather upon the living God who 'does not save with sword and spear' (17:47). Many of our problems in the Christian life stem from the fact that we lose sight of the greatness of God, and become preoccupied with the present troubles and struggles of life. These things may stand like a mighty Goliath before us, but if we are setting God before our eyes, then we will not fear or fall. David's words, in Psalm 16:8, explain the secret of his strength and courage: 'I have set the LORD always before me; Because He is at my right hand I shall not be moved.'

c) A further temptation which could have demoralized David's spirit, was the attitude of Eliab, his elder brother. His anger and disdain for David is reflected in these words: 'Why did you come down here? And with whom have you left those few sheep in the wilderness? I know your pride and the insolence of your heart ...' (1 Sam. 17:28). Eliab's outburst could hardly have been sharper or more vitriolic than this! If anything was designed to make David feel useless and guilty, it was surely this criticism from his own brother. And yet, David was not deterred in his quest and zeal to serve God's cause. Some criticism is best ignored!

David's experience can also be the Christian's too. We may be determined to honour God within our families and yet, receive a similar kind of reaction from those who are our 'nearest and dearest'. They may misjudge our motives, resent our love for the Bible, and misunderstand our loyalty to Jesus and His Church. Our Lord warns of family members who may be at variance with those in the same household who follow Him: 'A man's enemies will be those of his own household' (see Matt. 10:34–38). Satan can stir up our loved ones to resent or ridicule us, simply because we want to live for God's glory. But the same God who enabled David to resist the temptation to sink into a 'slough of despond',[1] will keep and sustain us in all our particular trials.

d) Another possible cause for discouragement came with Saul's misguided act of cladding David in his own armour. After hearing David's impassioned reply to his warning that he was just a youth and no match for Goliath, Saul agreed to let him go and fight the giant. But he insisted on sending him with a coat of mail, a bronze helmet and a sword, all of which would have been far too cumbersome for the young shepherd boy. Saul's intentions may have been good by equipping him with all the protection he could possibly muster, but David knew that he needed more than human help to overcome such a strong enemy: 'The Lord, who delivered me from the paw of the lion and from the paw of the bear, He will deliver me from the hand of this Philistine' (v. 37).

The church today, as it engages in its spiritual warfare against the forces of darkness, still faces arguments which sound so reasonable and plausible. We are told that we no longer need the outdated and archaic method of 'preaching' in this modern age; the church needs to become hi-tech and shed the relics of the past; and do we even need church buildings anymore? Would it not be better if we all stayed at home and tuned into the latest religious podcast and engaged in discussions about our faith? Now, leaving aside the past restrictions on gathering for worship, and having to do things in a way which protected us from being infected by Covid-19 in 2020–22, the arguments above run contrary to the Word of God. For instance, the apostle Paul 'charged' Timothy to, 'Preach the word! Be ready in season and out of season. Convince, rebuke, exhort, with all long suffering and teaching. For the time will come when they will not endure sound doctrine …' (2 Tim. 4:2–3). Then Paul, writing to Titus, makes it clear that the way God chose to make known His Word was 'through preaching' which was committed to him, 'according to the commandment of God our Saviour' (Titus 1:3). And then, if we are in any doubt about the importance of gathering for worship, let Hebrews 10:24–25 dispel such doubts:

> And let us consider one another in order to stir up love and good works, not forsaking the assembling of ourselves together, as is the manner of some, but exhorting one another, and so much the more as you see the Day approaching.

Chapter 20

Jonathan's defeat of the Philistines

(1 Samuel 14:1–23)

Setting the scene

Jonathan, the eldest son of King Saul, is known principally for his friendship and loyalty to David—a loyalty that brought him into conflict with his father and sovereign. Although he was his father's heir and in line to succeed him as Israel's king, he was willing to remain deeply loyal to David, even though it meant risking the danger of Saul's furious anger and the threat of being dispossessed of his crown rights (1 Sam. 20:31). On such an occasion, when Jonathan defended David's innocence before his father, Saul became so infuriated that he hurled his spear at him! (20:30–33).

The Philistine threat

During the time of the Judges, the Israelites had to contend with the aggression and oppression of the Philistines. The Philistines were sometimes used by God to chastise the children of Israel for their faithless adoption of foreign gods (Judg. 10:6–7). Men like Shamgar and Samson were raised up as defenders of the people but, as the Philistine threat increased, the need of a strong military leader was felt in Israel.

Saul was anointed king by Samuel and, after his second year as king, he assembled a standing army of three thousand men. Of those, he took two thousand men to be with him at Michmash—a location in the territory of Benjamin. This was also the place where the Philistines had encamped against Israel, before moving out to the mountain pass of Michmash. The remaining one thousand men were assigned to Jonathan in Gibeah, and it was here that he attacked and destroyed a garrison of Philistines (1 Sam. 13:3). The news of this Philistine defeat quickly spread throughout their camp.

Saul then mustered his troops at Gilgal and the Philistine army, consisting of three thousand chariots, six thousand charioteers and numerous foot soldiers, camped at Michmash, east of Beth-Aven (meaning 'house of iniquity'). Fearing such a huge enemy, the men of Israel melted away, and hid in caves and anywhere that offered shelter and refuge (13:6). Meanwhile, Saul and his troops waited for Samuel in Gilgal, but grew impatient because he had been delayed, and so, Saul took upon himself the role of the prophet (v. 9). At the same time, Jonathan and his army remained in Gibeah, while the Philistine army encamped in Michmash. The Israelite army was greatly impoverished by having no proper weapons to fight with (v. 22). Only Saul and Jonathan had any decent weapons so, humanly speaking, the situation for Israel was dire in the extreme. But Israel's extremity was God's opportunity.

Jonathan defeats the Philistines

Some might think that Jonathan's exploit to attack a heavily armed detachment of Philistines, with just his armour bearer to support him, was quite foolhardy but others, with the knowledge of God's Word, see it very differently. Not only was it an exceptional act of courage, but it also brought about a startling and unexpected victory for the people of God.

Without his father's knowledge, Jonathan and his 'bodyguard' set out to cross over to the Philistine garrison. His words to his young companion resounded with trust and confidence: 'Come let us go over to the garrison of these uncircumcised; it may be that the LORD will work for us. For nothing restrains the LORD from saving by many or by few' (1 Sam. 14:6). The young man's reply was wonderfully positive: 'Do all that is in your heart. Go then; here I am with you, according to your heart' (v. 7). Crossing the steep-sided valley, and scaling the precipitous cliff face, would have taken the skills of a rock climber and the strength of a warrior. Jonathan then explained his plan to his companion:

> If they say thus to us, 'Wait until we come to you,' then we will stand still in our place and not go up to them. But if they say thus, 'Come up to us,' then we will go up. For the LORD has delivered them into our hand, and this will be a sign to us (vv. 9–10).

Sure enough, the Philistines invited them to come up to them, possibly thinking that they were Hebrew deserters. Then, in a surprise attack, the two daring Israelites killed at least twenty Philistines. What followed was a powerful intervention from the Lord. The earth shook, causing panic and confusion among the entire Philistine army (v. 15). Saul's lookouts in Gibeah witnessed the mystifying sight of this vast army melting away before their very eyes. Those Israelites who had previously deserted came out from their hiding places and many others, who had defected to the Philistines, now fought with Saul, and 'the LORD saved Israel that day' (v. 23).

Points for reflection

1] Knowing what we read of Jonathan's character, it would be natural for us to assume that he would have made an excellent successor to King Saul. In addition to this, the Lord's Word to Samuel concerning the identity of Israel's king: 'He may save My people from the hand of the Philistines' (1 Sam. 9:6), may have perhaps confirmed such an assumption. But Saul's successor would not be his natural heir, nor would it ultimately be the choice of Israel, but the choice of the 'King eternal ... who alone is wise' (1 Tim. 1:17). How wonderful to know that God's thoughts are not our thoughts, neither are our ways His ways! And the reason for this is to do with His infinite wisdom and holiness: 'For as the heavens are higher than the earth, So are My ways higher than your ways, And My thoughts than your thoughts' (Isaiah 55:8–9).

2] Jonathan's conviction that nothing could possibly hinder the Lord's power to save, was the major factor in his brave decision to encounter the Philistine garrison, with the aim of putting them out of action. This same conviction motivated the apostle Paul in his endeavours to make the gospel known, both to the Jewish and Gentile world of his day. The significant factor was always the power of God: 'For I am not ashamed of the gospel of Christ, for it is the power of God to salvation for everyone who believes, for the Jew first and also for the Greek' (Rom. 1:16). Satan consistently seeks to make us doubt and question the power of God, either with regard to our own personal lives or with respect to the life and activity of the Church. The reality is that '... nothing restrains the LORD from saving by many or by few' (1 Sam. 14:6).

3] Jonathan's armour-bearer played a vital role in the success of Israel's victory over the Philistines. He is one of those nameless individuals in the Bible who, by his faith and boldness, 'became valiant in battle, turned to flight the armies of the aliens' (Heb. 11:34). But, perhaps, an important lesson for us is the unity of purpose he displayed, being one in heart with Jonathan; and, because of this, Jonathan's arm was strengthened in his resolve to serve the Lord. Should this not be our calling too, that we might stand with, and encourage, those who are serving the Lord in their particular ministries, and be of one heart and mind in the work to make Christ known in every place?

David's conflict with the Amalekites

(1 Samuel 30:1–20)

Setting the scene

The raid on the town of Ziklag by the Amalekites, and the conflict which then ensued later between David and the invaders, took place towards the end of David's fugitive period. It was soon after these events that David was crowned king, first of all reigning at Hebron for seven years, and then at Jerusalem for the rest of his forty-year reign. In all of these incidents while awaiting God's time, he was being prepared for the privileged role of becoming Israel's king, invested with the authority of a vice-regent under God.

Ziklag, originally a town allotted to the tribe of Simeon, on the Philistine-Israelite border (Josh. 19:1–8), had become Philistine, belonging to Gath, whose king was Achish. David had fled to Achish from Saul's anger and was allowed by Achish to make it his refuge from Saul (see 1 Sam. 27:1–7).

The crisis at Ziklag

David and his men had returned to Ziklag, having been refused by the Philistine princes to join with their army against the Israelites. When they had arrived, they were met with a scene of devastation. The invaders had burnt the place to the ground, and had captured all the women and children, both young and old. This terrible scene caused David and his men to be overwhelmed with grief and tears (v. 4). The loss of David's two wives—and the wives of all his men and the loss of the many sons and daughters—was an incredible blow to the whole company. But what was particularly stressful for David was that the people's grief and anger turned to recrimination and the talk of stoning David for this catastrophic failure quickly circulated throughout the camp (v. 6).

David's response to the crisis

David's reaction to the disaster at Ziklag was seen in two main ways. The first was the way of faith and trust: 'But David strengthened himself in the LORD his God' (1 Sam. 30:6). He looked for strength, not in men or in himself, but in the Lord his God. Then a second reaction was the way of wisdom; he sought the Lord's guidance: 'So David inquired of the LORD, saying, "Shall I pursue this troop? Shall I overtake them?"' The answer from the Lord could not have been clearer. 'And He answered him, "Pursue, for you shall surely overtake them and without fail recover all"' (v. 8).

Following this confirmation from the Lord, David and his six hundred men set out on their mission to pursue and recover all the captives. On arriving at the Brook Besor (a stream southwest of Ziklag), two hundred of his men were so weary that they could not continue with the whole troop, and remained to rest at the Brook.

Then, in a remarkable act of providence, they came across a young Egyptian man who had been abandoned by the Amalekite forces. He was brought to David and given something to eat and drink, which helped to revive him. David then questioned him about his background and present circumstances. He told David that he had been a servant of an Amalekite and had been part of a troop of raiders who had been responsible for invading the territory of Judah, and in particular the town of Ziklag. But he had been deserted because he had fallen sick, and was left without food and water for three days (v. 12). Here was David's opportunity to gather intelligence about the whereabouts of the Amalekites and even be led there by this young man. After allaying the Egyptian's fears with regard to being killed by David's men, or handed over to his old master, he agreed to take David down to the camp of the Amalekites (v. 15).

The scene was one of revelry and celebration over the amount of spoil they had seized during their raids. They were completely unprepared for David's attack, which lasted from dusk to the evening of the next day. None were spared, apart from four hundred young men who escaped on camels. The Lord's words were wonderfully fulfilled: David had recovered everyone and everything that had been abducted by the raiders (vv. 16–19).

The aftermath

David, victorious in his mission to save all the captives, then returned to the two hundred men who had been too exhausted to join the rest of his troop. All of them went out to meet David and the people with him, and he warmly greeted them (v. 21). However, some of the more depraved of David's men were not willing to share any of the spoil that had been recovered with those who had stayed behind. But David would have none of it; those who stayed behind would not be excluded from sharing the spoils of battle, and he gave two reasons for his decision. Firstly, the victory in the battle must be attributed to the Lord rather than any human power: 'My brethren, you shall not do so with what the LORD has given us, who has preserved us and delivered into our hand the troop that came against us' (v. 23). Secondly, the men who had not actually fought in the battle still had an important part to play. They had been responsible for looking after the supplies and, therefore, enabled the fighting force to travel freely without being cumbered in any way (v. 24). Thus, David showed that he had been both humble in defeat and magnanimous in victory and was, in truth, 'a man after His [the Lord's] own heart' (1 Sam. 13:14).

Points for reflection

1] David's reaction to the disaster at Ziklag has much to say to all Christians who find themselves in arduous and demanding situations. We can imagine David's feelings of horror and shame as he arrived back at Ziklag and was met with such devastation. We can learn, however, from what David did not do in this harrowing situation. He did not begin to blame God for allowing this tragedy to take place. He did not attempt to vindicate himself by trying to defend himself before his men. Nor did he allow himself to be swallowed up by self-pity. These would have been the normal reactions of the natural heart, but David maintained his integrity and dignity by not reacting in the way his men did.

What David did do was to comfort or encourage himself in the Lord. His Psalms often describe the way he thought of God in times of great difficulty: 'Be my strong refuge, to which I may resort continually ...' (Ps. 71:3; see also 28:1; 62:2, 6). Any crisis in our lives always tests our character and, while we do not want them and never look for them, they do have their purpose.

> Now no chastening seems to be joyful for the present, but painful; nevertheless, afterwards it yields the peaceable fruit of righteousness to those who have been trained by it (Heb. 12:11).

2] As we reflect on the way David spoke to his grumbling and griping followers in verse 22, it reminds us of Paul's exhortation to the believers in Colosse: 'Let your speech always be with grace, seasoned with salt, that you may know how you ought to answer each one' (Col. 4:6).

David's motley band of followers are described as men who were in distress, in debt and discontented (1 Sam. 22:2). And yet, David calls them, 'My brethren', and graciously reasons with them. Our speech is important and ought to reflect the change that has taken place in our lives (Col. 3:8; Eph. 4:29). Our speech, according to the New Testament, ought to be gracious, interesting, sensible and, above all, pure.

3] David regarded God's guidance as something indispensable (vv. 7–8). He rejoiced to know that the Lord was willing and able to guide him: 'I will instruct you and teach you in the way you should go; I will guide you with My eye' (Ps. 32:8). Are we just as assured as David about God's promise of guidance, and do we see it as a privilege and a necessity for our lives in this troubled world?

> Lead us, O Father, in the paths of peace;
> Without Thy guiding hand we go astray,
> And doubts appall, and sorrows still increase;
> Lead us through Christ, the true and living Way.
> (William Henry Burleigh, 1812–71)

Chapter 22

The Battle of Mount Gilboa

(1 Samuel 28:3–19; 31:1–10)

Setting the scene

With the account of this battle, the first book of Samuel closes. It is, of course Saul's last battle, and the words of David to Abishai concerning Saul, have a remarkable poignancy: 'As the LORD lives, the LORD shall strike him, or his day shall come to die, or he shall go out to battle and perish' (1 Sam. 26:10).

Saul seeks guidance from a medium

The account of the battle is brief and factual and yet, it remains a moving record of the event. The Philistines assembled their armies in the Valley of Jezreel, camping at Shunem. They were preparing for a supreme victory over the forces of Israel, confident that they outnumbered and outpowered Saul's army. Israel had camped in the foothills of Mount Gilboa, which was a good defensive position. However, seeing the sheer size of the Philistine troops, Saul's 'heart trembled greatly' (1 Sam. 28:5), and being unable to receive any guidance from God, he left the camp at night and sought a medium at Endor. During this secret meeting, the deceased Samuel warns him of a crushing defeat at the hands of the Philistines. Moreover, both he and his three sons would lose their lives (vv. 15–25).

Saul dies by his own hand

On the next day, Saul and his forces are overwhelmed by the enemy, and compelled to make a humiliating escape from the scene of the battle. But, while being fiercely pursued by the Philistine chariots, Saul suffers a critical hit by a Philistine archer. Fearing he would be captured and abused, he quickly orders his armour-bearer to dispatch him with his sword. The man, however, fears killing the 'anointed of the LORD' (1 Sam. 24:6). Saul, therefore, reaches for a sword and falls on it, thus dying by his own hand (1 Sam. 31:3–6). His tragic suicide was the final act of a long process of self-destruction. Saul's worst enemy was not the Philistines, but himself.

On the following day, when the Philistines came to strip the dead, they found the bodies of Saul and his three sons. Saul's armour is removed from his body, and his head is severed and taken to the temple of Dagon as a trophy of war. His body, and the bodies of his sons, are fastened to the wall at Beth Shan (vv. 8–10). But, when the men of Jabesh Gilead hear of this humiliation, they travel at night and, at great risk to their own lives, rescue their bodies. After burning their corpses, their bones are buried under a tamarisk tree. In honour of Saul, the people of Jabesh Gilead then fast for seven days (vv. 11–13).

Points for reflection

1] Saul has been called a tragic hero, whose career was dogged by self-will and a spirit of envy towards David. He had never fully accepted that God had chosen David to replace him as king and it was, therefore, this stubborn defiance of God's will that led to such tragedy in his life and reign.

How vastly different was Jesus' attitude to God's will. Speaking of Himself as the Son of Man, with all the authority which that commanded, He stated that He did not seek His own will, but the will of His Father who sent Him (John. 5:30). Indeed, He made clear to His disciples that His 'food' or 'nourishment' was in carrying out the will of His Father (John 4:34). The ultimate expression and submission to His Father's will is found in His words at Gethsemane: 'O My Father, if this cup cannot pass away from Me unless I drink it, Your will be done' (Matt. 26:42). The writer to the Hebrews, in his closing benediction, reminds us of the vital importance of 'doing God's will':

> Now may the God of peace who brought up our Lord Jesus from the dead ... make you complete in every good work to do His will, working in you what is well pleasing in His sight, through Jesus Christ, to whom be glory forever and ever. Amen (Heb. 13:20–21).

2] The intensity of Saul's envy towards David acted like a cancer, eating its way through his life and reign as Israel's king. Both in our personal lives, and in the life of the Church, envy and strife must never be given a place to hide, or manifest itself in any form or shape. Sadly, the church at Corinth, with all its gifts and abilities, was allowing itself to be torn apart by factions and infighting. Paul describes their behaviour as being carnal:

> I fed you with milk and not with solid food; for until now you were not able to receive it, and even now you are still not able; for you are still carnal. For where there are envy, strife, and divisions among you, are you not carnal and behaving like mere men? (1 Cor. 3:2–3).

3] Saul's failure and defeat in this particular battle is ascribed to his unfaithfulness to the Lord:

> So Saul died for his unfaithfulness which he had committed against the LORD, because he did not keep the word of the LORD, and also because he consulted a medium for guidance (1 Chr. 10:13).

Unfaithfulness can manifest itself in various ways. In Saul's case, it chiefly revealed itself in his unteachable spirit, and his unwillingness to humble himself and listen to the counsel and admonition of Samuel. Among the many wise sayings of Solomon, these two are possibly the most apt with regard to King Saul:

> He who disdains instruction despises his own soul, but he who heeds rebuke gets understanding (Prov. 15:32).

> The fear of the LORD is the instruction of wisdom, and before honour is humility (15:33).

Not all the kings of Israel were unteachable! Josiah for instance received this lovely word from the Lord:

> Thus says the LORD God of Israel: 'Concerning the words which you have heard—because your heart was tender, and you humbled yourself before God ... I have also heard you (2 Chr. 34:26–28).

4] The whole matter of guidance in the Christian life can be a source of anxiety and frustration. However, we are given many promises in God's Word which, if trusted and acted upon, can be the antidote to worry and confusion. One such promise is stated by David in Psalm 32:

> I will instruct you and teach you in the way you should go; I will guide you with My eye. Do not be like the horse or like the mule, which have no understanding ... (Ps. 32:8–9).

It is always best to follow the counsel of the Lord, rather than the 'counsel of the ungodly' (Ps. 1:1).

The battle for Jerusalem

(2 Samuel 5:1–10)

Setting the scene

Despite the fact that part of Jerusalem was gained by Judah's forces at the time of the conquest (Judges 1:8), the stronghold itself had not been taken and was still under the control of the Jebusites (Judges 1:21). The first mention of Jerusalem, also known as Salem, is in Gen. 14:18, where we are told that Melchizedek, king of Salem, blessed Abraham after his victory over the captors of Lot. In the Egyptian Amarna letters, it is named as Urusalim, a city known for its military prowess and its strategic importance.

Having become King of a united Israel, David was now ready to make Jerusalem his capital by securing it from the Jebusites. David's path to the throne had been a troubled one, with long periods of exile and much harassment from Saul. But finally, in God's time, David became the long-awaited leader of His people. At the age of thirty, he became king of Judah and reigned for seven years at Hebron. His reign in Jerusalem over the united kingdom would last for thirty-three years; so in all, he served forty years as the shepherd king of God's people (v. 2).

The conquest of Jerusalem

The Jerusalem of David's day had been built on a rise with deep valleys surrounding it. With its strong wall, it had remained invincible for centuries and so, it is little wonder that the Jebusites were ready to meet David's men with taunts and mockery. Their boast was that, even if the 'blind and lame' were to defend their city, it would still be impregnable (2 Sam. 5:6).

This was, of course, a fatal underestimation of the strength and resolve of David's troops. The capture of the stronghold or citadel at the northern end of the city, was the first stage of the assault. This, however, had not given them access to the town itself, but David knew of a subterranean passage that led from the Gihon spring into Jerusalem, which would give his men the opportunity for a surprise attack on the heart of the city. He offered a challenge to anyone who would climb up 'the water shaft' and defeat the Jebusites. If they succeeded, he would make them the commander of his army. Joab took up the challenge and the seemingly unassailable city fell to David without much effort (vv. 8–10). He renamed Jerusalem as the 'City of David', thus establishing it as his own capital city, suitably placed between Judah and the northern tribes.

Points for reflection

1] Despite the Jebusites' arrogant confidence in their fortress walls, their stronghold was easily taken. It is a graphic illustration of the words of Proverbs 16.18: 'Pride goes before destruction, and a haughty spirit before a fall.' The Bible makes it clear that man's pride in his own accomplishments, intellectual or otherwise, is a particular evil. Its evil lies in the fact that it defies the essential nature of true wisdom which, according to God's Word, is 'the fear of the Lord':

> And to man He said, ' Behold, the fear of the LORD, that is wisdom, and to depart from evil is understanding' (Job 28:28).

2] The apostle Paul, writing to the Corinthians in his second letter, uses the term, 'strongholds', as a metaphor to describe those things on which human confidence rests and is established. The humanism, materialism and secularism of our day could well be described as the modern strongholds, which are against the knowledge of God. He reminds them that, in the spiritual conflict in which they are engaged, these 'strongholds' cannot be fought against with fleshly weapons, but rather the weapons that are essentially spiritual and powerful through God:

> For the weapons of our warfare are not carnal but mighty in God for pulling down strongholds, casting down arguments and every high thing that exalts itself against the knowledge of God ... (2 Cor. 10:4–5).

The proud arguments and pretensions of men, which exalt themselves against the knowledge of God, can only be defeated by the Word of God and through prayer. Only when the sinful heart is changed by the power of the Spirit, will there be a surrendering of these 'high things' and a thankful acceptance of the glorious knowledge of God. One of the many examples of this in the Scriptures is in the life of King Nebuchadnezzar. His testimony in the Book of Daniel reveals how the exalted knowledge he had of himself, and his achievements, was cast down by the power of God. Here, first of all, is the proud declaration of his self-confidence:

> The king spoke, saying, 'Is not this great Babylon, that I have built for a royal dwelling by my mighty power and for the honour of my majesty?' (Daniel 4:30).

But, after he is humbled by the Lord, his words are very different:

> Now I, Nebuchadnezzar, praise and extol and honour the King of heaven, all of whose works are truth, and His ways justice. And those who walk in pride He is able to put down' (4:37).

From pride to praise can only be possible by the conquering grace of God!

Chapter 24

Absalom's rebellion and defeat

(2 Samuel 18:1–18)

Setting the scene

This chapter describes the defeat and death of David's third son, Absalom. The passage ends with David's heartbreaking lament for his treacherous son: 'O my son Absalom—my son, my son Absalom—if only I had died in your place! O Absalom my son, my son!' (v. 33).

Absalom's treason had been in the planning for at least four years. He had been exiled by David for the murder of his half-brother, Amnon, who had raped Tamar (Absalom's sister). Following his return from exile, Absalom grew resentful towards his father for not allowing him the opportunity to see him. David may well have prevented the murder of Amnon had he acted swiftly to discipline his wayward son for his violation against Tamar. He might also have prevented Absalom's rebellion by agreeing to meet with him much sooner. Although David was a strong king, sadly he lacked the strength and resolve to discipline his two sons.

With the help and contrivance of Joab, David's chief commander, Absalom was given permission to return from his exile (see 2 Sam. 14). David then agreed to see his son Absalom, but it was too late for any meaningful reconciliation. Absalom had taken full advantage of his position as the king's son to charm the populous of Israel by offering them quick resolutions to their complaints and grievances. The inevitable result was that he 'stole the hearts of the men of Israel' (2 Sam. 15:2–6).

Within a short time, Absalom had gathered ample support from the people and had also succeeded in assembling an army of willing fighters. His next step was to boldly make himself king at Hebron—the place where David had ruled for seven years as king and the place which now became Absalom's city of revolt. The news of Absalom's insurrection quickly reached David, who ordered his servants to prepare for an immediate escape from Jerusalem: 'Arise, and let us flee, or we shall not escape from Absalom. Make haste to depart, lest he overtake us suddenly and bring disaster upon us, and strike the city with the edge of the sword' (2 Sam. 15:14). David clearly knew what Absalom was capable of.

Absalom's defeat and death

David's plan to quell Absalom's rebellion was to divide his troops into three divisions under the command of his three loyal commanders, Joab, Abishai and Ittai (2 Samuel 18:2). His intention was to lead the army himself, but his men strongly objected to this by saying that he was 'worth ten thousand' of them and that his presence in the city would be needed far more (2 Sam. 18:3). Before leaving for battle, the three commanders were instructed by David to 'Deal gently ... with the young man Absalom,' an order which was heard by all the people (v. 5). Much of the ensuing battle took place in the woods of Ephraim, which proved to be disastrous for Absalom's forces, and for Absalom himself. When encountering David's men, Absalom turned and escaped on his mule but, tragically, his head and hair became caught in the branches of a tree, and he was left hanging helplessly in the air. The news reached Joab that Absalom was now in this precarious and fateful position. Joab failed to understand why the messenger had not taken the opportunity to kill him there and then. The answer he received was a reminder of David's express command concerning Absalom: '... Beware lest anyone touch the young man Absalom!' (v. 12). However, it failed to impress Joab who swiftly went to end the pretender's life (9–15).

Points for reflection

1] It seems quite ironic that Absalom's healthy head of hair—a feature he must have been very proud of—proved to be his downfall (v. 9). There is much in the Scriptures that warns us against pride, or 'vainglory' which seems a better term to describe Absalom's case. Perhaps the most appropriate verse, with regard to this story, is Solomon's proverb: 'Pride goes before destruction, and a haughty spirit before a fall' (Prov. 16:18).

2] There are both good and bad elements in David's concern for Absalom.

a) Take, for instance, his command to the leaders of the army to 'Deal gently for my sake with the young man Absolom' (2 Sam. 18:5). We can fully understand that, as a father, David would not have wished any harm to have come to his son. His love for his wayward son is commendable. But was this command reasonable or unreasonable? Was it wise or foolish? Absalom had caused the death of many thousands of men in his bid to seize power in Israel. He had become a threat to David's kingship and a danger to the nation of Israel. As the leader of a rebellious army, he would have been the prime target and, therefore, David's request was lacking in judgement.

b) Then take Joab's behaviour in this incident. Was it good or bad to kill Absalom? Well, we could say it was bad to disobey an order given by the king of Israel, and yet we can also say that Absalom's death brought an end to the rebellion and to further bloodshed. Sometimes in life, issues are not always black and white. We may see two sides to a problem and they both appear to be valid. This is why the apostle James gives us such helpful advice: 'If any of you lacks wisdom, let him ask of God who gives to all liberally and without reproach, and it will be given to him' (James 1:5). There is, of course, a condition to this wonderful promise: 'But let him ask in faith, with no doubting, for he who doubts is like a wave of the sea, driven and tossed by the wind' (James 1:6). Faith and humility must go hand in hand when seeking the Lord's guidance.

3] David's betrayal by Absalom must have been one

of the hardest ordeals of his life. It reminds us of the grief Jesus must have felt when betrayed by Judas. David's prophetic words, in one of his Psalms, describes something of this grief: 'Even my own familiar friend in whom I trusted, who ate my bread, has lifted up his heel against me' (Ps. 41:9). The account of Christ's betrayal is particularly poignant:

> Now His betrayer had given them a sign, saying, 'Whomever I kiss, He is the One; seize Him.' Immediately he went up to Jesus and said, 'Greetings, Rabbi!' and kissed Him. But Jesus said to him, 'Friend, why have you come?' (Matt. 26:48–50).

Betrayal of any kind can be a most distressing thing, but the comfort for those who are in Christ is that His love is unchanging and eternal and will never let us down.

4] David's reluctance and delay to meet with Absalom face to face, when he had returned to Jerusalem from exile, was a mistake. It did little to bring about a true reconciliation between himself and his erring son. Christ's teaching in the 'Sermon on the Mount' gives us clear guidance as to our behaviour towards a 'brother or sister' who has something against us:

> Therefore if you bring your gift to the altar, and there remember that your brother has something against you, leave your gift there before the altar, and go your way. First be reconciled to your brother,

> and then come and offer your gift. Agree with your adversary quickly, while you are on the way with him ... (Matt. 5:23–25).

The emphasis, here, seems to be on making sure that you are reconciled with your brother without too much delay. If we agree with our brother quickly, there is less likely to be prolonged resentment and future trouble. This quote, from Arthur W. Pinero, is suitably pithy and succinct: 'If you have a thing to pardon, pardon it quickly. Slow forgiveness is little better than no forgiveness.'[1]

Chapter 25

The rebellion of Sheba

(2 Samuel 20:1–26)

Setting the scene

Once again, David faced the menacing forces of insurrection—not this time from his own family but from the family of Israel, a rebel Benjamite named Sheba. In order to understand the rebellion of Sheba, we must try to analyse the quarrel between Israel and Judah.

Trouble within the family of Israel (2 Samuel 19:9–15)

Following Absalom's defeat and death, there was much confusion among the tribes of Israel about David's return to Jerusalem. When and who would bring him back from exile? No one seemed to be taking the initiative to recall him and, although many in Israel had backed the usurper Absalom, there was a general consensus that the king should be recalled. This all reached the ears of David but, instead of welcoming the change of allegiance by the northern tribes, he chose to rebuke the elders of Judah for their reluctance and delay in receiving him back. The message he sent via his two priests, Zadok and Abiathar, was uncompromising:

> Why are you the last to bring the king back to his house, since the words of all Israel have come to the king, to his very house? You are my brethren, you are my bone and flesh. Why then are you the last to bring back the king? (2 Sam. 19:11–12).

This telling-off proved to be successful and so, they arranged to meet the king at the Jordan for a formal ceremony to welcome him back. But only Judah, the king's own tribe, were officially invited to meet the king and to bring the king over the Jordan. The effect of this partisanship caused deep resentment among the northern tribes, and they bitterly complained that the king had been 'stolen' from them (v. 41). Judah responded by dismissing the charge of favouritism, or of receiving any kind of financial reward from the king. The men of Israel answered that they had the largest share in David's kingship and, what was more, they were the first to advise bringing the king back. (2 Sam. 19:42–43) All of this rancour between Israel and Judah, gave Sheba the opportunity to proclaim himself as the new leader of a break away Israel: 'We have no share in David, nor do we have inheritance in the son of Jesse; every man to his tents, O Israel!' (20:1).

Those who championed Saul's dynasty and had wanted to see it continue, were very much behind their new national hero, Sheba. But, just as Absalom's failed attempt to make himself king led to his downfall and ruin, so also Sheba's effort to gain the glory for himself would be doomed from the beginning. Joab, having now recovered his position as the chief commander of David's forces by killing Amasa, pursued Sheba and those who followed him to a city called Abel, in the region of Beth Maacah (20:9–13).

A wise woman's intervention

Sheba had sought refuge in Abel, a city in northern Israel. The safety he sought would be very short-lived because the forces of Joab had arrived and had set about making a siege mound against the city (v. 15). In no time, the wall of the city was being battered, but a woman suddenly appeared from the city wall wanting to speak to Joab and crying, 'Hear, hear! Please say to Joab, "Come nearby, that I may speak with you"' (v. 16). Joab felt constrained to listen to her as she reasoned with him on behalf of her city. She firstly reminded him that Abel was a city known for its reputation as being judicious and wise, and for sorting out disputes. Why, then, should he destroy a city known for its wisdom? (v. 18). In the second place, she told him that it was a city whose inhabitants were peaceable and faithful. Would it make sense to punish a people who were loyal to Israel? And finally, she argued that the city was 'a mother in Israel', a guide and example to other towns and cities, and to destroy it would be to 'swallow up the inheritance of the LORD' (v. 19).

Joab was suitably convinced by this woman's passionate defence of her city and explained that his intention was not to 'swallow up or destroy' the city (v. 20), but to seize a man who had 'raised his hand against the king, against David' (v. 21). If the people of the city would deliver such a traitor to him, he promised to depart from the city. The woman then went and exercised her reasoning powers—this time to all who lived in Abel—and Sheba's head was thrown down to Joab. This was enough for Joab to withdraw from the city and to return victorious to Jerusalem (v. 22).

Points for reflection

1] It is regrettable that David missed the opportunity to unify the kingdom by showing grace and generosity to those tribes that had been duped by Sheba. Instead, he drove a wedge between Judah and the rest, by encouraging tribal factions and loyalties. The truth that 'the best of men are men at their best' is apposite here.

Writing to Timothy, Paul gives him some serious pastoral advice about the danger of showing favouritism: 'I charge you before God and the Lord Jesus Christ and the elect angels that you observe these things without prejudice, doing nothing with partiality' (1 Tim. 5:21). James, likewise, warns his readers of bringing the faith of the Lord Jesus Christ into disrepute by showing partiality to those who are rich and well clothed:

> For if there should come into your assembly a man with gold rings, in fine apparel, and there should also come in a poor man in filthy clothes, and you pay attention to the one wearing the fine clothes and say to him, 'You sit here in a good place,' and say to the poor man, 'You stand there,' or, 'Sit here

> at my footstool,' have you not shown partiality among yourselves, and become judges with evil thoughts? (James 2:2–4).

James exposes the snobbish conduct of some members of the congregation, there in Jerusalem. But what about us? Are we from the fixation of regarding people for what they have, rather than for what they are?

2] This wise, but nameless, woman's intervention in a time of crisis is an encouragement to us in the matter of prayer:

a) Her boldness in approaching Joab is something which gains his ear and attention. The writer to the Hebrews assures us that, having been cleansed from our sins, we can have boldness '... to enter the Holiest by the blood of Jesus, by a new and living way which He consecrated for us, through the veil, that is, through His flesh ... let us draw near with a true heart in full assurance of faith ...' (Heb. 10:19–22).

b) Her humility also stands out, as she expresses her inferior position: 'Hear the words of your maidservant', to which he willingly replied, 'I am listening' (2 Sam. 20:17). When we come as humble children to our sovereign King, we can be assured that He says to us, 'I am listening.' His word through Isaiah confirms this: 'But on this one will I look: on him who is poor and of a contrite spirit, and who trembles at My word' (Isa. 66:2).

c) Then there is the way she pleads for her people as 'a mother in Israel', and as the 'inheritance of the LORD' (2 Sam. 20:19). It is a lovely example of fervent intercession for those she loved. It is both our duty and privilege to be intercessors for those inside and outside the Church of the Lord Jesus Christ. Paul exhorts Timothy, '... that supplications, prayers, intercessions, and giving of thanks be made for all men, for kings and all who are in authority, that we may lead a quiet and peaceable life in all godliness and reverence' (1 Tim. 2:1–2).

But our greatest example of intercessory prayer must surely be Christ Himself who '... bore the sin of many, and made intercession for the transgressors' (Isa. 53:12). As His people's great High Priest, 'He always lives to make intercession' for us (Heb. 7:25).

Chapter 26

The battle against the giants

(2 Samuel 21:15–22)

Setting the scene

This brief passage records David's victories over the Philistine giants. David's military career had begun when, as a youth, he answered the challenge to fight Goliath, the giant of Gath. His victory brought him the admiration of King Saul and his son, Jonathan, and a place in the royal court (1 Sam. 17–18). Now, at the end of his military era and as King of Israel, he is still fighting giants!

The giants of the Bible

The first mention of 'giants' is in the Book of Genesis:

> There were giants [Nephilim] on the earth in those days, and also afterward, when the sons of God came in to the daughters of men and they bore children to them. Those were the mighty men who were of old, men of renown (Gen. 6:4).

There is some debate as to the origin of these 'giants'. On the one hand, there are those who interpret the phrase, 'sons of God', as meaning fallen angels who had taken wives from the women of the day; and from these unions there came this race of giants called the Nephilim, who are described as the men of renown. Others dispute this interpretation and are not convinced that this race of giants should be traced to these angel marriages. One such advocate for an alternative view is J. Barton Payne who writes: 'Evangelicals who are committed to the unity and credibility of Scripture ... generally identify the sons of God with the godly portion of the descendants of Seth who involved themselves in indiscriminate mixed marriages.'[1] Whatever the origin of these giants, their presence on the earth greatly contributed to the spread of wickedness in the world and to the further depravity of the human race (Gen. 6:5–7).

When, later, Moses sent spies to explore the land of Canaan, they came back with the daunting news that:

> The land through which we have gone as spies is a land that devours its inhabitants, and all the people whom we saw in it are men of great stature. There we saw the giants ... and we were like grasshoppers in our own sight, and so we were in their sight (Num. 13:32–33).

The reference to Og, king of Bashan (Deut. 3:11), who is described as a 'remnant of the giants', has this fascinating detail about his bed: 'Indeed his bedstead was an iron bedstead. ... Nine cubits is its length and four cubits its width ...' [13.5 feet long by 6 feet wide]. The region of Bashan was called 'the land of the giants', and these people were known as the Anakim. An additional name given for these men of great stature is found in the book of Deuteronomy: 'The Emim had dwelt there [Moab] in times past, a people as great and numerous and tall as the Anakim. They were also regarded as giants, like the Anakim, but the Moabites call them Emim' (Deut. 2:10–11).

Philistine giants destroyed

Once again, the Philistines made war with Israel and a giant named Ishbi-Benob, a descendant of Goliath, made a concerted effort to kill the elderly David, who had become exhausted during the battle. This was possibly the closest David got to being killed on the battlefield. Abishai, one of his chief officers, came to his aid and fatally struck the giant; this intervention by his trusted friend saved David from certain death (2 Sam. 21:15–17). This episode convinced David's men that it was time for the King to retire from fighting any more battles. The risk of losing the 'lamp of Israel' was too great. Instead, David would wait to hear of the accomplishments of men like Sibbechai, Elhanan, and Jonathan who, with great courage, dispatched the rest of the giants. (vv. 20–22).

Points for reflection

1] We may ask if there is any significance in the fact that giants troubled David right to the end of his life? The answer to this must be 'Yes!' From the conflict with Goliath, at the beginning of his military career, to the fight with the Philistine giants when an old man, these giants were seen as the enemies of God's people, and especially as the enemy of the anointed leader of Israel.

They symbolized the strong opposition that David faced throughout his life, but an opposition that the Lord often delivered him from: 'He delivered me from my strong enemy, from those who hated me; for they were too strong for me. They confronted me in the day of my calamity, but the LORD was my support' (2 Sam. 22:18–19). And, just as David knew the protection of the Lord from such fierce and monstrous enemies, so we today may know the abiding presence of the Holy Spirit as we confront those forces that are too strong for us alone (Eph. 6:10–18).

2] As we read of these giants being slain, we can only admire the courage of those who fought them. Throughout the New Testament we are exhorted to be courageous in our fight of faith:

> Watch, stand fast in the faith, be brave, be strong (1 Cor. 16:13).

> Fight the good fight of faith, lay hold on eternal life (1 Tim. 6:12).

> You therefore must endure hardship as a good soldier of Jesus Christ (2 Tim. 2:3).

> Why should I fear the darkest hour,
> Or tremble at the tempter's power?
> Jesus vouchsafes to be my tower.
> Though hot the fight, why quit the field?

Chapter 27

Why must I either fly or yield,
Since Jesus is my mighty shield?
(John Newton, 1725–1807)

The battle to defend Samaria

(1 Kings 20:1–22)

Setting the scene

Ahab, Israel's seventh king was one of the worst kings to reign over the nation of Israel. The Bible's introduction to him, in 1 Kings 16:29–30, makes this abundantly clear, where it describes him as the 'son of Omri [who] did evil in the sight of the LORD, more than all who were before him'.

Ahab had made Samaria his capital and had built a luxurious palace which he had adorned with ivory (1 Kings 22:39). He had also, in defiance of the Lord, erected a temple for the 'Tyrian Baal', and by this he '... did more to provoke the LORD God of Israel to anger than all the kings of Israel who were before him'(1 Kings 16:33). His infamous wife, Jezebel, was very much a co-partner in provoking the Lord's anger and, together, they must rank as the most degenerate pair of Israelites who ever occupied a place of leadership in Israel.

The Syrian threat

Ben-Hadad of Syria, along with a huge coalition of his allies, made up of thirty-two kings, decided to attack Samaria. All these military forces, including horses and chariots, surrounded Samaria. Messengers were then sent to remind Ahab that Syria was the dominant power, and that the city with all his 'loveliest wives and children' belonged to Ben-Hadad (1 Kings 20:3). Ahab's reply seems to indicate his complete subordination to Ben-Hadad: 'My lord, O king, just as you say, I and all that I have are yours' (v. 4). A further humiliation came when the messengers are sent back a second time and the demands of Ben-Hadad become significantly more menacing: not only is Ahab to surrender his wives and children to the king, but he is to stand by while the king's servants search his house, plus the houses of his servants, and seize everything of value (vv. 5–6).

Greatly alarmed by these threatening demands, Ahab calls for all his advisors. They counsel him not to 'listen or consent' to Ben-Hadad's further demands. Ahab then sends the messengers back with these words: 'Tell my lord the king, "All that you sent for to your servant the first time I will do, but this thing I cannot do"' (v. 9). Ahab may have hoped that this would have appeased Ben-Hadad and have averted the worst possible outcome. But a third message from the Aramean king reached Ahab, threatening him with the utter destruction of the city and its inhabitants (v. 10). Surprisingly, this declaration of war was met with a plucky little proverb from Ahab: 'Tell him: "One who puts on his armour should not boast like one who takes it off"' (v. 11, NIV). The proverb has been given a more modern interpretation: 'Preparing for a war is one thing, winning it is quite another.' In a more colloquial form, it may be rendered, 'Don't count your chickens before they hatch.'

A word from the Lord

Without wasting any more time, Ben-Hadad ordered his servants to prepare for a general assault on Samaria. But, quite suddenly, into this sequence of events entered a prophet of the Lord who assured Ahab of certain victory: 'Thus says the LORD: "Have you seen all this great multitude? Behold, I will deliver it into your hand today, and you shall know that I am the LORD' (v. 13). This intervention by God was to convince wayward Ahab that the Lord is the true God and that He alone is able to deliver Israel from the enormous army Ben-Hadad had assembled against them. The prophet also instructed Ahab how the victory would be accomplished (v. 14). The battle plan was to send a relatively small force of 232 young men who probably would have formed the bodyguards of the provincial governors. Then, there would be a larger force of 7000 Israelite soldiers, who would follow the select group of 'commanders' as they advanced towards the enemy camp.

The first division of soldiers began their advance at midday, while Ben-Hadad and the thirty-two kings were in their tents getting drunk. The scouts that had been sent out by Ben-Hadad reported back that a small force of men was coming out of Samaria and Ben-Hadad treated the news of their approach with ridicule (v. 18). If he had thought that this group of men had been sent as a delegation seeking terms of peace, he was gravely mistaken. With the Israelite army joining them, 'each one killed his man' and the Syrian army panicked and fled from the battle (v. 20). Ben-Hadad himself escaped on a horse with some of his horsemen, but the king of Israel overpowered the horses and the chariots, killing most of the Syrian army (v. 21).

Points for reflection

1] Neither Ahab nor the Israelites deserved this victory, which had been a clear intervention by the Lord who, in His faithfulness, chose to be gracious towards His disobedient people. Ahab had not sought God's help in this crisis and yet, despite his faithless neglect in prayer, the Lord remained faithful to the nation. Matthew Henry makes this poignant comment: 'God was gracious to Ahab, that He might magnify His mercy in doing good to one so evil and unthankful.'[1] God can be gracious to us at any time and in any condition, as these words of Isaiah make clear:

> Therefore the LORD will wait, that He may be gracious to you; And therefore He will be exalted, that He may have mercy on you. ... Blessed are those who wait for Him (Isa. 30:18).

2] In this incident, we see how God chose to work through a limited number of men, with a limited amount of experience in warfare. Those who are called to 'fight the good fight of faith' (1 Tim. 6:12) are also weak in themselves for such a calling. Paul, writing to the Corinthian church, states that:

> For you see your calling brethren, that not many wise according to the flesh, not many mighty, not many noble, are called. But God has chosen the foolish things of the world to put to shame the wise, and God has chosen the weak things of the world to put to shame the things which are mighty; and the base things of the world and the things that are despised God has chosen, and the things which are not, to bring to nothing the things that are, that no flesh should glory in His presence (1 Cor. 1:26–29).

Although the preaching of the Gospel seems to be weak and foolish to many, and is even despised by some, it is the way God has chosen and ordained to build His Church in the world:

> For since, in the wisdom of God, the world through wisdom did not know God, it pleased God through the foolishness of the message preached to save those who believe (1 Cor. 1:21).

3] The Israelites had their directions for this battle, not from a capricious Israelite king, but from an inspired prophet. We, today, are privileged to have the inspired

Word of God to instruct us and teach us in the way we should go (Ps. 32:8). We are not to look to the world's shifting standards or follow the latest social trends, but rather let the 'lamp' and 'light' of the Bible lead us along the path of life (Ps. 119:105).

Chapter 28

Asa and the battle against Zerah the Ethiopian

(2 Chronicles 14:9–15)

Setting the scene

Asa was one of Judah's finest kings. This was all the more significant and gratifying since both his father and grandfather were unfaithful and ungodly 'shepherds' of God's people. The contrast is made clear as Asa is introduced to us in 2 Chr. 14:2: 'Asa did what was good and right in the eyes of the LORD his God.' His reign began by reforming the evil practices of these earlier kings. He removed the altars and shrines of all the false deities that had been adopted by Judah and even deposed Maachah, his depraved 'queen mother', for setting up an obscene image of Asherah (14:3–5; 15:16). So, during the first ten years of his rule, Judah enjoyed a period of peace and rest, which Asa recognized as being the result of God's favour and blessing:

> Therefore he said to Judah, 'Let us build these cities and make walls around them, and towers, gates, and bars, while the land is yet before us, because we have sought the LORD our God; we have sought Him, and He has given us rest on every side' (14:7).

Asa defeats Zerah

During this time when 'the kingdom was quiet under him' (14:5), Asa wisely strengthened Judah's army (v. 8). With Benjamin's forces as well, the army totalled 580,000. This was an act of great foresight for, before too long, the nation would be forced to defend itself against the enormous armed forces of Zerah the Ethiopian (v. 9). Equipped also with 300 chariots, Zerah's army came to Mareshah—a town in the lowland of Judah, which had been fortified by Rehoboam, Asa's grandfather. Asa's troops went out to engage with the enemy in the Valley of Zephathah at Mareshah. Realizing that the odds were against them in terms of the sheer numbers of the enemy, Asa turned to God in prayer and said:

> 'LORD it is nothing for You to help, whether with many or with those who have no power; help us, O LORD our God, for we rest on You, and in Your name we go against this multitude. O LORD, You are our God; do not let man prevail against You!' (v. 11).

Asa's prayer was wonderfully and miraculously answered: 'So the LORD struck the Ethiopians before Asa and Judah, and the Ethiopians fled' (v. 12).

The writer of Chronicles gives us no indication as to exactly how the Lord struck the opposing army but leaves us in no doubt that it was a mighty intervention on His part, which brought an abrupt end to Zerah's aggression. All that Judah had to do now was to pursue the fleeing army, who were completely overthrown and utterly broken, so that any recovery would be impossible (v. 13).

Points for reflection

1] Asa's resolute attitude towards Israel's idolatry, and his action to remove all traces of false worship, even from his own household, revealed his zeal and love for God. This work of 'reformation', that took place in Asa's day, has its parallel in the Christian life. While conversion only takes place once, the transforming work of the Holy Spirit is an ongoing work as we are 'being transformed into the same image from glory to glory, just as by the Spirit of the LORD' (2 Cor. 3:18). We are, of course, co-workers with the Spirit and, as Paul states in his letter to the Philippians, we are to 'work out your own salvation with fear and trembling; for it is God who works in you both to will and to do for His good pleasure' (Phil. 2:12–13). The great difference in this 'reformation' is that it is both an inward and outward change. The natural man, whose life is lived without the influence of the Holy Spirit, never really changes. But the question we must ask ourselves as Christians is, are we just as ruthless as Asa in dealing with the idols of our own lives? Cowper's hymn puts it so well:

> The dearest idol I have known, whate'er that idol be, help me to tear it from Thy throne, and worship only Thee.[1]

2] Asa's love for God is not only seen in his attempt to reform the religious life of Judah, but also in his personal trust and dependence upon Him. This is seen supremely in his prayer before the battle against the Egyptian multitude: '... help us, O LORD our God, for we rest on You, and in Your name we go against this multitude' (14:11). Asa's trust was not a substitute for inaction, since he was willing 'to go' against the enemy, but his eyes were not focused on his 'mighty men of valour', or upon 'shields' and 'spears', but upon the Lord his God. Dependence upon God is a sign of maturity in the Christian life, rather than immaturity. The more we learn to lean and rely on our heavenly Father, the more we grow in spiritual wisdom and maturity. This is especially reflected in the life of the Lord Jesus: as a youth He '... increased in wisdom and stature, and in favour with God and men' (Luke 2:52). As a man He always spoke and acted according to His Father's will: 'For I have not spoken on My own authority; but the Father who sent Me gave Me a command, what I should say and what I should speak' (John 12:49).

3] Like so many instances in Israel's military victories, this victory against an Ethiopian invasion, demonstrated that One greater than a human leader had taken over as 'commander of the army'. The language of the chapter speaks for itself: 'The LORD struck (defeated) the Ethiopians'; 'they were broken before the LORD and His army'; 'the fear of the LORD was upon them' (14:12, 13, 14). What a comfort to know that in our fight against sin, the devil and the world, One greater than all these put together is within us: 'You are of God, little children, and have overcome them, because He who is in you is greater than he who is in the world' (1 John 4:4).

> Why should I fear the darkest hour,
> or tremble at the tempter's power?
> Jesus vouchsafes to be my tower.
>
> Against me earth and hell combine;
> but on my side is power divine;
> Jesus is all, and He is mine!
> (John Newton, 1725–1807)

Jehoshaphat's battle at Jeruel

(2 Chronicles 20:1–30)

Setting the scene

Jehoshaphat came to the throne in Judah after the reign of Asa, his father, who was one of the finest kings of Judah. During Jehoshaphat's reign, he enjoyed a long period of rest and peace, giving him the opportunity to carry out various religious reforms in Judah, with the purpose of establishing a true and vital worship in the land. His crowning epitaph was that 'The LORD was with Jehoshaphat'. Jehoshaphat followed in his father's spiritual footsteps in the sense that '... he walked in the former ways of his father David; he did not seek the Baals, but sought the God of his father, and walked in His commandments ...' (2 Chr. 17:3–4). He too was renowned for bringing the people back to a more faithful walk with God, setting up leaders and judges who he commanded to 'act in the fear of the LORD, faithfully and with a loyal heart' (2 Chr. 19:9). And, like his father Asa, he too enjoyed a season of peace, during which he was empowered to establish the kingdom of Judah: 'So Jehoshaphat became increasingly powerful, and he built fortresses and storage cities in Judah' (2 Chr. 17:12). During this stage in his reign, he also enlarged his army by attracting many of the 'mighty men of valor', who came willingly to serve their king (2 Chr. 17:14–19).

Jehoshaphat faces a powerful enemy

The inevitable time came when Jehoshaphat faced the

threat of war by an alliance of Judah's enemies, Moab, Ammon and Edom: a 'great multitude ... from beyond the sea' (2 Chr. 20:2). These nations had been spared from being destroyed by the Israelites at the time of the conquest of the land of Caanan (20:10). This sudden aggression against Judah was particularly callous, considering they had been graciously treated by Israel. Jehoshaphat's initial response to this huge menace was to 'fear', but it was not a fear that paralysed him and made him incapable of any meaningful response. Immediately, he 'set himself to seek the LORD, and proclaimed a fast throughout all Judah' (20:3). Judah's reaction was a whole-hearted willingness to follow Jehoshaphat's call to fast and pray and so, all the men with their wives and children converged at Jerusalem.

The scene was now set for the King to lead his people in prayer, and we can imagine the stillness and silence which fell upon the whole assembly as Jehoshaphat lifted up his voice to pray. The prayer wonderfully exalted the Lord, as he spoke of God as the ruler 'over all the kingdoms'(v. 6), and reminded the people of their privileged position as 'His people Israel'(v. 7). He also mentioned God's gracious promise to hear and save His people when they 'cry out to You in our affliction'(v. 9). His prayer ended with the humble acknowledgement that they 'have no power against this great multitude that is coming against us, nor do we know what to do, but our eyes are upon You' (v. 12).

Strictly speaking, Jehoshaphat had a considerable army with many skilled fighters, but his prayer demonstrated that his entire dependence was upon God Himself, rather than upon any human strength and ability.

God hears and answers

The Lord's voice, in answer to Jehoshaphat's prayer, is heard through Jahaziel, who is described as one of the sons of Asaph. The Spirit gives him the authority to proclaim the message of victory over their enemies. Not only are they not to fear the massive company that has come against them, but they will not need to fight in this battle, '... for the battle is not yours, but God's' (20:15, 17). And yet, there is the command to, '... go down against them' (v. 16), which is just as significant and pressing as the command to '... stand still and see the salvation of the LORD ...'. Jehoshaphat's reaction to this prophecy is to bow in reverent submission, which gave the lead for 'all Judah and the inhabitants of Jerusalem' to do the same (v. 18).

The enemy is vanquished

Jehoshaphat's battle cry, in verse 20, is an exhortation to all in Judah and Jerusalem, to have faith in God, and in His prophets, with the promise that if they do so, they would 'be established' and would 'prosper'. He then appointed a choir of singers to lead in praise as the army moved forward and, while they praised the Lord, the victory came in the most unexpected way. As they arrived at the watchtower of the wilderness, they found that their enemies had destroyed one another, and their lifeless bodies were scattered over the earth. They then returned with great rejoicing, bearing the abundant spoils of war with them (vv. 22-30).

Points for reflection

1] Jehoshaphat's fervent prayer must have been both a comfort and a challenge to the people assembled at Jerusalem. It would have been a comfort, in that it would have awakened their memories of God's majestic power and faithfulness to His people in past generations. Added to that, it would have renewed their hope in God's covenant promises to save them from all kinds of disasters, including sword and judgment. And then, of course, it would have been a challenge to their faith, simply because their king openly confessed that they had no power or plan against such an enemy!

As we pray, in the company of our brothers and sisters in Christ, are we mindful of these two elements in prayer? Firstly, to comfort one another by reminding ourselves of the glorious characteristics of our Lord: His faithfulness and greatness, and His unchanging love for His people. But then, we must acknowledge our utter dependence upon God, by confessing that we have no power in ourselves to affect any real change, either in the world or in the Church. This is the challenge of trust and faith, to say with Jehoshaphat, '... nor do we know what to do, but our eyes are upon You (v. 12).

2] Jehoshaphat enjoyed the full support of a united community, who had surrounded him with their love and concern. Those who are called to minister to God's people need to know the love and support of their flock. There is nothing more encouraging for a pastor than to know that the church he serves is united in their concern for the glory of God, and for the wellbeing of His servant. Conversely, there is nothing more discouraging for a pastor than to have to deal with a spirit of back biting and disunity among the members of the church.

3] The song of praise played a major part in Judah's deliverance. It was clearly pleasing to the Lord to see His people marching forward with praise in their hearts and upon their lips. The place of praise is not to be underestimated in the believer's life: 'Whoever offers praise glorifies Me' (Ps. 50:23). While an unbelieving world robs God of praise, 'let the saints be joyful in glory; ... let the high praises of God be in their [our] mouth' (Ps. 149:5–6).

4] Throughout the history of the children of Israel, their victories over their enemies have often come in a most unexpected way: none more so, than Jehoshaphat's triumph at Jeruel. How wonderful to know that God's help and blessing can come in unexpected ways! As Dr D.

Martyn Lloyd-Jones put it, 'this surely is the romance of the Christian life'.[1] We never quite know when or how God will work, so let us not foolishly predict or expect the Lord to work according to our little schemes and programmes!

> We rest on Thee, our Shield and our Defender!
> Thine is the battle; Thine shall be the praise.
> (Edith Adeline Cherry, 1872–97)

Chapter 30

The Battle of Beth Shemesh

(2 Chronicles 25:17–24)

Setting the scene

When the nation of Israel was not fighting other nations, they were engaged in fighting themselves. The conflict described in this chapter is just one of those 'domestic' battles of the divided kingdom: Israel in the north and Judah in the south. The two kings involved were Amaziah, king of Judah, and Joash, king of Israel. Sadly, most of these kings of both Israel and Judah fell far short of what God had required them to be.

This particular battle is a perfect illustration of Isaiah's comments on the pride of men: 'The lofty looks of man shall be humbled, the haughtiness of men shall be bowed down, and the LORD alone shall be exalted in that day' (Isa. 2:11). The culprit with the haughty spirit, in this case, was Judah's king, Amaziah. His name means, 'Jehovah is mighty', but regrettably, he was not a man that lived up to such a sacred and distinctive title. He was half-hearted in his loyalty to the Lord and ended up drifting completely away from Him (2 Chr. 25:2, 14–15).

Amaziah challenges Joash to a fight

Having sought the advice of his advisors, Amaziah sent this challenge to Joash: 'Come, let us face one another in battle' (v. 17). Quite why he did this is not explicitly mentioned in the passage, but there could have been two strong possible reasons: firstly. his victory over Edom may have gone to his head and given him an inflated view of the strength of his army, and of his own prowess in battle. Such conceited thinking would have led him to throw the gauntlet down to Israel (see 2 Chr. 25:5–16). A second possible reason for Amaziah's rash challenge could have been Joash's refusal to agree to a marriage between his daughter and Amaziah's son, which would have offended Amaziah's pride. It may well have been that both of these things induced Amaziah to propose such a reckless challenge.

Joash's response

Joash's response comes in the form of a parable, which is stated in verses 18–19. It was designed to bring Amaziah to his senses and to leave him in no doubt as to the foolishness of his provocation. Amaziah was a mere 'thistle', who had proudly demanded that the 'cedar's' daughter be given to the 'thistle's' son in marriage. The inevitable outcome of such arrogance would be the crushing of the thistle! However, Joash also elucidates the parable by warning that Amaziah's challenge is nothing else but a swollen-headed proposal, which will be to his own loss and humiliation:

> Indeed you say that you have defeated the Edomites, and your heart is lifted up to boast. Stay at home now; why should you meddle with trouble, that you should fall—you and Judah with you? (v. 19).

In other words, Amaziah is to be content with his triumph over Edom and not look for further trouble!

Amaziah's downfall

Amaziah's refusal to listen to the advice of Joash to 'stay at home' resulted in them both facing each other at Beth Shemesh (house of the sun), a town in Judah. The account of the battle is limited in detail. However, we know that Amaziah suffered a humiliating defeat. His men fled to their tents, while Amaziah himself was taken captive and brought back to Jerusalem. Although he was spared death, he nevertheless suffered a massive blow to his pride and reputation as a successful warrior king.

We can trace the chain of causes of Amaziah's downfall, which God allowed. In verse 20, the writer states, 'But Amaziah would not heed ...'. His refusal to listen to sound advice was the first factor in his fool-hardy attempt to make war with Israel. His greatest mistake, however, was to refuse to heed God's Word, by setting up the gods of Edom on Israelite soil and bowing down before them. This brought God's judgement upon him personally, and upon the nation. As well as Amaziah's unteachable spirit, we have his restlessness in seeking yet another conflict with his neighbour. The most impossible thing for Amaziah was to 'stay at home' and be satisfied with things as they were!

Points for reflection

1] Joash warned Amaziah not to 'meddle with trouble' (v. 19). Solomon's humorous proverb poignantly cautions those who are inclined to meddle in other people's affairs: 'He who passes by and meddles in a quarrel not his own is like one who takes a dog by the ears' (Prov. 26:17). The risk in meddling in someone else's business is two-pronged: it will anger that person, and it will do harm to the meddler. The risk in meddling in someone else's business has harmful consequences for both parties involved. Paul had to warn certain Christians in Thessalonica, who were lazy 'busybodies' and who were walking in a 'disorderly manner', to 'work in quietness and eat their own bread'. This behaviour was clearly dishonouring the Lord Jesus Christ (2 Thes. 3:11–12). And the apostle Peter, writing to Christians who were suffering for their faith, distinguished between suffering as a Christian and suffering as 'a busybody in other people's matters' (1 Peter 4:15).

2] Amaziah's arrogant presumption was a chief fault in his character, which led inevitably to his ruin. Jeremiah gives us the perfect description of the 'natural heart': 'The heart is deceitful above all things, and desperately wicked; who can know it?' (Jer. 17:9). The only answer to this 'heart condition', is found in Paul's glorious statement in his second letter to the Christians at Corinth: 'Therefore, if anyone is in Christ, he is a new creation; old things have passed away; behold, all things have become new' (2 Cor. 5:17). The 'natural heart' must be replaced by 'the new heart', which is the work of the Holy Spirit alone (John 3:5–8).

3] Amaziah's gradual drift away from God reveals the peril of a half-hearted loyalty to Christ. Rarely does the Christian become a backslider overnight. Typically, it is a gradual and almost surreptitious decline in faithfulness towards Christ and His Word. Jude gives us the antidote to such a decline: 'But you, beloved, building yourselves up on your most holy faith, praying in the Holy Spirit, keep yourselves in the love of God, looking for the mercy of our Lord Jesus Christ unto eternal life' (Jude 1:20–21).

4] Had Amaziah found the secret of contentment, he would have spared himself much distress and sorrow. But departing from God meant that he was also departing from godliness which, according to the apostle Paul, is both the companion and secret of contentment (1 Tim. 6:6).

Jehoram and the Moabite campaign

(2 Kings 3:1–27)

Setting the scene

Following the death of Ahab, his eldest son, Ahaziah, became king of Israel (2 Kings 3:2). King Ahaziah's reign came to an abrupt end, when he was seriously injured from falling 'through the lattice of his upper room in Samaria' (2 Kings 1:2). He had no son to succeed him and so Jehoram, Ahab's second eldest son, became king. Jehoram followed in the footsteps of his notorious parents, Ahab and Jezebel, earning the familiar epithet, 'And he did evil in the sight of the LORD' (v. 2).

Mesha throws off the yoke of Israel

The Moabite king, Mesha had been paying a yearly tribute to Israel during Ahab's reign as king. Within a few years of Jehoram's reign, Mesha refused to continue to pay the required tribute of wool and rams and rebelled against Israel (vv. 4–5).

Jehoram's furious response was to quickly assemble an army and attack the rebellious Moabite king. Jehoram was aware that to successfully invade Moab he needed the support of Jehoshaphat, king of Judah. Not simply because a joint alliance with Judah would greatly strengthen his campaign, but he also needed Jehoshaphat's permission for his forces to march through the territory of Judah (v. 7). Jehoshaphat gladly agreed to support Israel's war against Moab: firstly, because Moab had been a mutual enemy of Judah and Israel; and secondly, Jehoshaphat considered the unity of Judah and Israel to be an important factor for future relations. His words in reply to Jehoram's request show a warm unanimity:

> And he said, 'I will go up; I am as you are, my people as your people, my horses as your horses' (2 Kings 3:7).

The battle plan

Jehoshaphat, however, was anxious to know Jehoram's battle plan: 'Which way shall we go up?' he asked. The answer given by Jehoram may have surprised Jehoshaphat: 'By way of the Wilderness of Edom' (v. 8). The obvious route would have been a more direct approach, crossing the River Jordan and then into the north of Moab. The march on this 'round-about route' took seven days, as it passed through Edom on its way down to the south of Moab. The advantage of arriving in the south was that they would be attacking Moab in the rear—the weakest area of defence. The king of Edom and his troops may have joined the two forces during their march through his territory as the Bible makes mention of three kings from this point on in the passage. But, after a week's march through the desert, the situation with the supply of water became desperate. With no water for the men and their animals, Jehoram cried out in despair: 'Alas! For the Lord has called these three kings together to deliver them into the hand of Moab' (v. 10). Jehoshaphat reacted differently, and asked for the help of a prophet: 'Is there no prophet of the LORD here, that we may inquire of the LORD by him?' (v. 11). One of Jehoram's servants reported that Elisha would be a convenient prophet to contact, and Jehoshaphat had the confidence to know that he was a man who would speak with the authority of the Lord (v. 12). All three kings, then made their way down to where Elisha was staying.

Elisha enters the scene

On arriving there, Jehoram is given a cold reception by Elisha, who rebukes him by saying, 'What have I to do with you? Go to the prophets of your father and the prophets of your mother' (v. 13). This stern rebuke is directly aimed at Jehoram and, therefore, Elisha agrees to help only for the sake of king Jehoshaphat (v. 14). He calls for a harpist, and while he is playing, Elisha is given a word from the Lord. They are directed to make the valley full of ditches in readiness for the Lord's provision of an abundance of water, which would flow from Edom without even a sign of rain or wind (v. 17). Not only would the water save them from certain disaster, but it would mislead the Moabites into thinking that its red appearance, caused by the reflection of the sun, was the blood of their enemies (vv. 22–23). Their mistake in thinking that Jehoram's forces had turned upon their allies, resulted in their destruction and defeat. Mesha's frenzied and evil act of sacrificing his own son to Moab's god, brought the campaign to an abrupt end, with the victors returning to their own land (v. 27).

Points for reflection

1] In this incident the characters of Jehoram and Jehoshaphat are clearly revealed when under stress. When the water runs out, Jehoram's reaction is to resort to sarcasm and blame. The Lord is charged with being responsible for bringing the three kings together, only to kill them with thirst or let them be slaughtered by the Moabites (v. 13). Jehoshaphat, on the other hand, looks to God. He neither jumps to hasty conclusions or rushes to blame God but is willing to wait and listen to what the Lord has to say through His prophet. He is also ready to obey the Lord's word when it is revealed through His servant Elisha.

These two different reactions bring to light the spiritual state of each of these two kings. Jehoram's hasty action, in attributing blame to God, is a sign of an unregenerate heart. Soon after the fall, Adam was quick to blame Eve for his sin, but the greater evil was to try to lay the blame on God: 'Then the man said, "The women whom You gave to be with me, she gave me of the tree, and I ate"' (Gen. 3.12). The heart of man has not changed since the fall and is still '... deceitful above all things, and desperately wicked' (Jer. 17:9).

Jehoshaphat, with all his shortcomings, was a man with a renewed heart. The nature of his heart is described in 2 Chr. 17:6: 'And his heart took delight in the ways of the Lord.' In faith, he waits for God to speak, and trusts when he cannot see. 'Now faith is the substance of things hoped for, the evidence of things not seen' (Heb. 11:1).

2] The situation in which Judah and Israel found themselves in, seemed hopeless and impossible. How could they possibly survive without water? But God, in His grace, turned this situation to one of hope and victory. The heaven-sent water came in fulfillment to the promise given through Elisha.

Jesus gives life-giving water to all who believe in Him. He turns the self-filled life, with all its thirst and unrest and with all its spiritual need, into a life characterized by hope, peace and joy. The woman of Samaria had left her water pot to run back to her village with the greatest news in the world: 'Come, see a Man who told me all things that I ever did. Could this be the Christ?' (John 4:29). If ever there was a woman, whose life was characterized by hopelessness and unrest, it was her (John 4:17–18). But she, and many of her fellow Samaritans, found in Christ the answer to their spiritual thirst: that 'fountain of water springing up into everlasting life' (John 4:14).

3] Elisha's words to Jehoram are strikingly relevant for us today. After telling him how the Lord would miraculously provide water for all to drink, he then says,

'And this is a simple matter in the sight of the LORD ...' (2 Kings 3:18). Elisha points to the all-sufficiency of the Lord to provide for all our needs and, in doing so, challenges the quality and reality of our trust in Him. Paul, writing to the Christians at Corinth, assures them of God's boundless grace to meet all their needs: 'And God is able to make all grace abound toward you, that you, always having all sufficiency in all things, may have an abundance for every good work' (2 Cor. 9:8).

> Jesus, Jesus, all sufficient,
> Beyond telling is Thy worth;
> In Thy Name lie greater treasures
> Than the richest found on earth.
> Such abundance
> Is my portion with my God.
> (William Williams, 1717–91)

Chapter 32

Syria's army captured

(2 Kings 6:8–23)

Setting the scene

This remarkable incident took place during the ministry of Elisha and the reign of Jehoram, king of Israel. Syria was one of Israel's worst enemies, and this event occurred while Aram was the Syrian king, having proclaimed war against Israel. The part Elisha played in this particular conflict is pivotal. He is 'the man of God' who passed on vital information to Jehoram about the plans and movement of the Syrian forces (vv. 8–9). With this military intelligence, Israel is warned of Syria's hostile intentions, and this took place on a number of occasions (v. 10). While we are not told exactly how Elisha received this information, we can safely say it was part of his supernatural ministry as God's prophet.

This, of course, was a source of great irritation and annoyance to the Syrian king. In his desperation, he called for his top officials and said to them, 'Will you not show me which of us is for the king of Israel?' (v. 11). In other words, 'who is the mole that is secretly betraying us?' The reply of his advisors is laced with incongruity and farce: 'None my lord, O king; but Elisha, the prophet who is in Israel, tells the king of Israel the words that you speak in your bedroom' (v. 12). It is obvious that his advisors were inferring Elisha had extraordinary powers and was an extremely dangerous threat to the king. In response to this worrying revelation, King Aram ordered his servants to go and see where Elisha could be found. The result was that they discovered Elisha in Dothan (v. 13).

King Aram's attempt to capture Elisha

The King left nothing to chance, and sent his cavalry and chariots, as well as a huge army, and they arrived at night in Dothan. When Elisha's servant awoke and went out of the house, he encountered the alarming sight of the city surrounded by Syrian forces. Terrified, he quickly alerted his master: 'Alas, my master! What shall we do?' (v. 15). Elisha's answer is wonderfully comforting: 'Do not fear, for those who are with us are more than those who are with them' (v. 16). But, although Elisha could see the unseen heavenly host surrounding them, the servant's eyes were closed to such a glorious reality and spectacle. So, Elisha prayed, 'LORD I pray, open his eyes that he may see' (v. 17). This is followed by another prayer, as the Syrian army approached the two men: 'Elisha prayed to the LORD, and said, "Strike this people, I pray, with blindness"' (v. 18).

With the Syrian army having been completely disarmed by this blindness, Elisha now advances out to meet them. Elisha informs them that they have come to the wrong city and, if they follow him, he will lead them to the man they are seeking. When they arrived at Samaria, the northern capital of Israel, Elisha prayed that the Lord would open their eyes and, with their vision restored, they saw that they were now the captives of Israel (vv. 19–20). Although it was in the power of the king of Israel to kill this enemy army and, although it may have been his wish to do so, he turned to Elisha to ask him if this was what he should do: 'My, Father, shall I kill them? Shall I kill them? (v. 21). Elisha's answer was unequivocal: 'You shall not kill them. Would you kill those whom you have taken captive with your sword and your bow?' Instead of killing them, he is to treat them humanely as prisoners of war: 'Set food and water before them, that they may eat and drink and go to their master' (v. 22). The outcome of this gracious action by Jehoram was the cessation of further raids by the Syrians into Israel's territory (v. 23).

Points for reflection

1] Just as the secret plans of the Syrian court were known to Elisha, so the devices of Satan are known to God. The devil can do nothing 'under cover' since God has revealed his 'stratagems' in the Scriptures. Paul could write to the Corinthians and say, '... we are not ignorant of his [Satan's] devices' (2 Cor. 2:11). Again, Paul could warn these Christians at Corinth who were being beguiled by false teachers that '... Satan himself transforms himself into an angel of light' (2 Cor. 11:13–14). The more we imbibe God's Word into our thinking, the more we will be enabled to be wise to his devices.

2] Just as Syria's army was disarmed by the power of God, we can rejoice that Christ, by His mighty death on the cross, 'having disarmed principalities and powers, He made a public spectacle of them, triumphing over them ...' (Col. 2:15). Paul gives us a magnificent description of our deliverance from sin and judgement when writing to the Christians at Colosse:

> And you being dead in your trespasses and the uncircumcision of your flesh, He has made alive together with Him, having forgiven you all trespasses, having wiped out the handwriting of requirements that was against us, which was contrary to us. And He has taken it out of the way, having nailed it to the cross (Col. 2:13–15).

3] Twice, Elisha prays for eyes to be open.

First of all, his servant needed to see God's protecting grace in order to be rid of his fear. Faith is always the answer to the 'torment' of fear, because it gives us a clearer understanding of our circumstances and enables us to see them in the light of God's Word. When we 'walk by faith, not by sight', we see things in the right perspective (2 Cor.5:7).

But then, the Syrians needed their eyes opened to their helplessness and captivity. It is God's work alone to open the eyes of those held captive by sin. Christ came to 'proclaim liberty to the captives, and recovery of sight to the blind' (Luke 4:18).

4] Elisha showed great kindness to the captive Syrians.

Matthew Henry makes this poignant comment: 'The most glorious victory over an enemy is to turn him into a friend.'[1] The incident has, however, an important principle to teach us. God's purpose was to show both Syria and Israel that national security ultimately depended, not on military force or strategy, but on the Lord. It is a tragic fact that the nations of the world, with their long history of conflict and wars, have been completely blind to this truth.

> Unless the LORD builds the house, they labour in vain who build it; Unless the LORD guards the city, the watchman stays awake in vain (Ps. 127:1).

Hezekiah's victory over Sennacherib

(2 Kings 18–19; 2 Chronicles 32:1–23; Isaiah 36:1–37:38)

Setting the scene

Hezekiah was one of the few kings of Israel who was exemplary both in faith and in godliness. He is introduced to us as one who:

> ... trusted in the LORD God of Israel, so that after him was none like him among all the kings of Judah, nor who were before him. For he held fast to the LORD; he did not depart from following Him, but kept His commandments, which the LORD had commanded Moses (2 Kings 18:5–6).

Such unclouded praise is not given lightly! This, of course, is not to say that Hezekiah was without his faults and failings, but it does reveal his deep aspiration to do 'what was right in the sight of the LORD, according to all that his father David had done' (18:3).

The other king mentioned in this story is Sennacherib, king of Assyria. The Assyrian meaning of his name is, 'Sin has increased the brothers', and he, like his predecessors before him, was an inveterate enemy of Israel. The Lord's words spoken to rebuke him, describe his arrogance and recklessness: 'Whom have you reproached and blasphemed? Against whom have you raised your voice, and lifted up your eyes on high? Against the Holy One of Israel' (Isa. 37:23).

Sennacherib's campaign against Judah

The Assyrian campaign against Judah began in the

fourteenth year of Hezekiah's reign. The significance of this is stated in the opening verse of 2 Chronicles 32: 'After these deeds of faithfulness, Sennacherib king of Assyria came and entered Judah; he encamped against the fortified cities, thinking to win them over to himself.' The 'deeds of faithfulness', referred to here, were the religious reforms Hezekiah carried out during those years (2 Kings 18:4–7). We can see the goodness and providence of God in giving Hezekiah this period of time to establish these much-needed changes to the religious life of Judah, before the onset of a possible war with the nation's enemies. But Sennacherib's ruthless campaign against the fortified cities of Judah, awakened in Hezekiah a sense of terror and doom and, conscious of a possible tragedy, he sent a message to Sennacherib expressing his regret in withholding tribute payments to Assyria. In his submission, he agreed to accept whatever terms of tribute Sennacherib would demand. Indeed, he went beyond what Sennacherib exacted from him, even stripping off the gold from the doors and pillars of the temple (2 Kings 18:14–16).

But now, in the fifteenth year of his reign, and after these years of intensive reformation, Hezekiah is ready to resist the imminent threat of invasion by Sennacherib. He sets out to secure Jerusalem's water supply from the invaders by channeling the water through a tunnel, from the Spring of Gihon to the Pool of Siloam. In addition to this, he strengthens the fortifications around the city and organizes a strong military defence by appointing competent military leaders. But these actions were not considered enough for Hezekiah, since resistance against such a powerful enemy had also to be a matter of faith and trust in the Lord his God. So, gathering together the 'captains of the people', Hezekiah exhorted them to be 'strong and courageous' in the face of Sennacherib's menacing threats of invasion. They could be confident in the knowledge that, although his army may have been a 'multitude' in number, it was only 'an arm of flesh' in reality, compared with the truth that the Lord their God was their present help, and would fight their battles' (2 Chr. 32:4–8). Hezekiah's words were the means of strengthening and encouraging all the people who were about to suffer Sennacherib's siege.

Messengers sent to intimidate the inhabitants of Jerusalem

While Sennacherib himself was engaged in besieging the city of Lachish (thirty miles south-west of Jerusalem), he sent envoys to Hezekiah with the aim of grinding down any confidence or belief that the people had of divine help. A fuller picture of the Assyrian attempt to frighten and undermine the Judean's trust in the Lord is given in 2 Kings 18:17–37. The chief spokesman, named 'the Rabshakeh' (chief minister), aimed his taunts and bluster at the inhabitants of Jerusalem (the people living on or in the region of the wall), rather than the three-man delegation Hezekiah had sent to negotiate with Sennacherib's emissaries. Knowing that the people would better understand him if he spoke in Hebrew, rather than in the diplomatic language of Aramaic, he began his blasphemous scorn and insults, which centred on four main deceptions:

- Firstly, Hezekiah's plans to resist the Assyrian siege were futile and useless, since he had no military might to do so (2 Kings 18:20).
- Secondly, the Lord in whom they trusted could not save them, any more than had the gods of other cities saved their adherents from the power of Assyrian forces. Therefore, they were not to let Hezekiah persuade them otherwise (vv. 29–35).
- Thirdly, if they looked to Egypt for help that would be both delusive and dangerous, since Egypt was just a 'broken reed ... on which if a man leans, it will go into his hand and pierce it' (v. 21).
- Fourthly, Judah's invasion had been sanctioned by the Lord. Therefore, Sennacherib had every right to destroy Jerusalem (v. 25). The response of the people was one of silence: '...the people held their peace and answered him not a word; for the king's commandment was, "Do not answer him."' (v. 36). It appears that this silence was not the response of

abject fear, but an obedient effort to carry out the orders of their king.

Hezekiah's response

The three men, Eliakim, Shebna and Joah, who were sent to negotiate with the Rabshakeh, returned to Hezekiah with their clothes torn, looking visibly shaken and distressed (v. 37). When the king listened to their report, he too 'tore his clothes, covered himself with sackcloth, and went into the house of the Lord' (Isa. 37: 1). He then sent a delegation of priests, including two of his chief advisors—Eliakim and Shebna—to Isaiah the prophet. In their distress and grief, they brought Hezekiah's anguished message:

> Thus says Hezekiah: 'This day is a day of trouble, and rebuke, and blasphemy ... it may be that the LORD your God will hear all the words of the Rabshakeh ... and will rebuke the words which the LORD your God has heard. Therefore, lift up your prayer for the remnant that is left' (2 Kings 19:3–4).

The reply from the prophet was wonderfully reassuring:

> And Isaiah said to them, 'Thus you shall say to your master, "Thus says the LORD: 'Do not be afraid of the words which you have heard, with which the servants of the king of Assyria have blasphemed Me. Surely I will send a spirit upon

> him, and he shall hear a rumor and return to his own land; and I will cause him to fall by the sword in his own land'"' (2 Kings 19:6–7).

However, as well as calling upon Isaiah to pray about the crisis, Hezekiah himself also implored the Lord to act and save them from the hand of the Assyrians. The letter which had come from Sennacherib, repeating all the contemptable language used by his messengers, is now taken into the house of the Lord, and 'spread before' Him. Hezekiah's plea is that the Lord would see and hear the situation that Jerusalem faces and act to save them from Sennacherib's hand. But the prayer is much more than a cry for help; it is a prayer that exalts the name of God, and glories in His unique sovereignty as the Creator of the heavens and earth. He alone is God, and Hezekiah desires that all the kingdoms of the earth may come to know this when the Lord delivers His people (2 Kings 19:15–19).

Sennacherib's defeat and death

It is important to see the contrast between the word spoken by the Lord concerning the prevention of Sennacherib's plan to enter and overthrow Jerusalem, and Sennacherib's boastful words written in his annals and on what is known as 'Sennacherib's Prism'.

The Word of the Lord given to his prophet Isaiah reads:

> Therefore, thus says the Lord concerning the king

> of Assyria: 'He shall not come into this city, Nor shoot an arrow there, Nor come before it with shield, Nor build a siege mound against it. By the way that he came, By the same shall he return; And he shall not come into this city,' says the LORD. 'For I will defend this city, to save it, For My own sake and for My servant David's sake' (2 Kings 19:32–34).

Sennacherib's Prism reads:

> But as for Hezekiah, the Jew, who did not bow in submission to my yoke, forty-six of his strong walled towns and innumerable smaller villages in their neighbourhood I besieged and conquered by stamping down earth-ramps and then by bringing up battering rams ... he himself [Hezekiah] I shut up like a caged bird within Jerusalem, his royal city.

It is clear that Sennacherib believed his siege around Jerusalem, and the subsequent surrender and humiliation of its king and people, would be a foregone conclusion. God, however, had other plans for Sennacherib. In answer to the prayers of Isaiah and Hezekiah, the Lord delivered the city by sending 'an angel who cut down every mighty man of valor, leader and captain in the camp of the king of Assyria' (2 Chr. 32:21). This powerful intervention of the Lord is described without any details of how this huge army was killed, but what we are told is that it happened suddenly during just one night and the grisly evidence of dead bodies was seen the next morning (2 Kings 19:35). Then, in deep shame, Sennacherib returned to Nineveh, where later he was assassinated by two of his sons—Adrammelech and Sharezer—who fled to eastern Turkey, the land of Ararat. He was succeeded by his other son, Esarhaddon.

Points for reflection

1] Hezekiah's acts of religious reform were urgently accomplished in accordance with the requirements of God's Word and were, for that reason, an important factor in preparation for the crisis he was soon to face. The cleansing of the House of the Lord, and the restoration of the Passover were the acts of a spiritually minded king and signified a genuine turning back to God. As Hezekiah honoured the Lord in these things, so the Lord honoured him by bringing about such a miraculous deliverance. As God's people, when we seek more and more to bring our lives into conformity with God's Word and will, we shall be the better prepared for all the varied circumstances of life. The wisdom of the Book of Proverbs repeatedly emphasizes this truth:

> But whoever listens to me will dwell safely, and will be secure, without fear of evil (Prov. 1:33).

> My son ... Keep sound wisdom and discretion; so they will be life to your soul and grace to your neck.

> Then you will walk safely in your way, and your foot will not stumble (Prov. 3:21–23).

2] Hezekiah's reforming zeal would not have been very popular with certain people in Judah, who would have been unhappy to see the 'high places' and the false 'altars' being destroyed (2 Kings 18:22). As Christians, we should not expect to be popular if we are fervent about our faith and devotion to the Lord Jesus Christ. Sadly, there will be those of a nominal faith within our churches, who criticize Christians whose fervency and commitment to the life of the church is very different from their own. The Lord warned of 'tares' growing among the 'wheat', and we may expect that in every true church there are those 'planted' by the devil who, for all outward appearances, seem to be true members of the fellowship of God's people (see Matt. 13:36–43).

3] Sennacherib would have seemed to his enemies, and to human judgement, a monstrous conqueror, who was incapable of being defeated. But, Isaiah, who saw him with the eyes of faith, considered him as a man who would soon be greatly humbled and punished by the God whom he had so blatantly blasphemed (Isa. 37:29). We too, must learn to look at the world situation with the eyes of faith and see the events of men always in relation to God.

Asaph the Psalmist acknowledged how he had temporarily lost his spiritual perspective, when he grew envious of the ungodly, who were doing well and becoming rich. Their arrogance and seemingly untroubled lives caused him to question his own struggles to live a godly life. But then, his view of all this changed the moment he 'entered the sanctuary of God', because it was there that he saw things in the light of God's truth: 'Surely You set them in slippery places; You cast them down to destruction. Oh, how they are brought to desolation, as in a moment!' (Psalm 73:18–19). This brought him to confess his foolish ignorance but, also, to praise the Lord for His unchanging love and faithfulness toward him:

> I was so foolish and ignorant; I was like a beast before You. Nevertheless, I am continually with You; You hold me by my right hand. You will guide me with Your counsel, and afterward receive me to glory (Psalm 73:22–24).

4] This incident contrasts the lies and deception of Sennacherib, with the honesty and humility of Hezekiah. Paul exhorts the Christians at Ephesus to 'put on the whole armour of God', so that they would be enabled to 'stand against the wiles of the devil.' Among his many wiles, is his work to deceive mankind, and especially those who trust in the Lord Jesus Christ. This is why Paul describes the first piece of armour as 'truth': 'Stand therefore, having girded your waist with truth ...' We are to use truth and truthfulness as we stand against the 'father of lies', just as our Saviour did when tempted by Satan in the wilderness (see Ephesians 6:10–19; Matt. 4:1–11).

CONCLUSION

The primary focus on this series of Old Testament battles has been to understand the lessons we may learn, as we engage in spiritual warfare in this 'present evil age' (Gal. 1:4). By considering those involved in these conflicts, and the things that motivated them, we can discern whether their actions were to the honour and glory of God, or purely for self- aggrandizement. We can discover how, in the face of overwhelming odds, God's servant's triumphed, despite their human frailty. The words of the writer to the Hebrews captures the essence and cause of their victories:

> By faith the walls of Jericho fell down after they were encircled for seven days ... and what more shall I say? For the time would fail me to tell of Gideon and Barak and Samson and Jephthah, also of David ... who through faith subdued kingdoms ... escaped the edge of the sword, out of weakness were made strong, became valiant in battle, turned to flight the armies of the aliens (Heb. 11:30–34).

A vital item in the 'whole armour of God' is the 'shield of faith' which, according to Paul, is to be 'taken up'– in other words, to be actively exercised by the believer against the 'wiles of the devil' (Ephesians 6:10–16).

A further lesson to be learnt from the conflicts of the

Old Testament is the prayerful dependency of those godly kings who were 'valiant in battle'. A wonderful example is found in Hezekiah's prayer in response to Sennacherib's arrogant threats against Jerusalem:

> And Hezekiah received the letter from the hand of the messengers and read it; and Hezekiah went up to the house of the LORD, and spread it before the LORD. Then Hezekiah prayed before the LORD, and said: 'O LORD God of Israel, the One who dwells between the cherubim. You are God, You alone, of all the kingdoms of the earth ... save us from his hand, that all the kingdoms of the earth may know that You are the LORD God, You alone' (2 Kings 19:14–19).

If we are to stand firm against the wicked accusations of the devil, we need to cultivate a humble dependency on the Lord, '... praying always with all prayer and supplication in the Spirit, being watchful to this end with all perseverance and supplication for all the saints ...' (Eph. 6:18).

SELECT BIBLIOGRAPHY

Baldwin, Joyce, *1 and 2 Samuel, Tyndale Old Testament Commentaries*, (Westmont, Illinois: IVP, 1988).

Barton Payne, J., *The Theology the Older Testament*, (Grand Rapids, Michigan: Zondervan, 1975).

Cundall, Arthur E. and Morris, Leon, *Judges and Ruth, Tyndale Old Testament Commentaries*, (Westmont, Illinois: IVP, 1974).

Edersheim, Alfred, *Bible History Old Testament*, (Peabody, Massachusetts: Hendrickson Academic, 1994).

Henry, Matthew, *Matthew Henry's Commentary on the Whole Bible*, Church, Leslie F., [Editor], Broad Oak Edition, (London: Marshall Pickering, 1973).

Herzog, Chaim and Gichon, Mordechai, *Battles of the Bible*, (London: Book Club Associates, 1978).

Hess, Richard S., *Joshua: An Introduction and Commentary [Tyndale Old Testament Commentaries]*, (Westmont, Illinois: IVP, 1996).

Wilcock Michael, *The Message of Chronicles*, (Westmont, Illinois: IVP Academic, 1987).

Wiseman, Donald J., *1 and 2 Kings: An Introduction and Commentary [Tyndale Old Testament Commentaries]*, (Westmont, Illinois: IVP, 1993).

ENDNOTES

Ch. 2 Moses and the Battle of Rephidim

1 Alfred Lord Tennyson, 'Idylls of the King', *The Coming of Arthur*, https://wmpl.org/quote/more-things-are-wrought-by-prayer/

Ch. 8 The campaign against Ai (1)

1 Custance, Arthur C., cited in: Blanchard, John, *Gathered Gold: A Treasury of Quotations for Christians*, (Welwyn Garden City: Evangelical Press, 1984), p. 305.

2 Ibid.

Ch. 9 The campaign against Ai (2)

1 Source unknown

Ch. 10 The Battle of Gibeon

1 Source unknown.

2 Archer, Gleason L., *Encyclopaedia of Bible Difficulties*, (Grand Rapids, Michigan: Zondervan, 1982), p. 161.

Ch. 12 Ehud and the campaign against the Moabites

1 Cundall, Arthur E. and Morris, Leon, *Judges and Ruth: Tyndale Old Testament Commentaries*, (Westmont, Illinois: IVP Academic, 2008), p. 79.

Ch. 15 Abimelech's conspiracy

1 Source unknown

2 https://www.ewtn.com/catholicism/library/saint-augustine-of-hippo-5207

3 https://www.gracegems.org/Brooks/a_string_of_pearls9.htm

Ch. 17 Samson's victory over the Philistines

1 Douglas, J. D., *The New Bible Dictionary*, (Westmont, Illinois: Inter-Varsity Press, 1982), p. 1133.

Ch. 18 The Ark of God captured

1 Source unknown.

Ch. 20 David and Goliath

1 The 'slough of despond' was a boggy swamp that comes from the book, *The Pilgrim's Progress* by John Bunyan. 'This can be rephrased as the "bog of depression". In spiritual terms, this is the condition of the would-be believer who is overcome by a conviction of sin—an overpowering sense of guilt and helplessness. In an extreme form, it can have a paralyzing effect on the individual.' *Understanding The Pilgrim's Progress*, (Leominster: Day One Publications, 2023), p. 29.

Ch. 25 Absalom's rebellion and defeat

1 https://www.preceptaustin.org/forgiveness-quotes-and-illustrations

Ch. 27 The battle against the giants

1 Payne, J. Barton, *The Theology of the Older Testament*, (Grand Rapids, Michigan: Zondervan, 1980), p. 206–207.

Ch. 28 The battle to defend Samaria

1 Henry, Matthew, *Matthew Henry's Commentary on the Whole Bible*, Church, Rev. Leslie F., [Editor], Broad Oak Edition, (London: Marshall Pickering, 1973), p. 392–394.

Ch. 29 Asa and the battle against Zerah the Ethiopian

1 From the hymn, 'O for a closer walk with God', by William Cowper (1731–1800).

Ch. 30 Jehoshaphat's battle at Jeruel

1 Lloyd-Jones, D. Martyn, *Preaching and Preachers*, (Grand Rapids, Michigan: Zondervan, 1971), Chapter 15, 'The Pitfalls and the Romance', p. 283.

Ch. 33 Syria's army captured

1 Henry, Matthew, *Matthew Henry's Commentary on the Whole Bible*, Church, Leslie F., [Editor], Broad Oak Edition, (London: Marshall Pickering, 1973), p. 408 (Under 1V).